# BEHIND CARTEL LINES

*Also by Stephen Bentley*

**The Steve Regan Undercover Cop Thrillers**

*The Secret*

*Duplicity*

*Dilemma*

*Rivers of Blood*

*Redemption*

*Bloodline Vendetta*

*The Final Betrayal*

**The Detective Matt Deal Thrillers**

*Mercy*

*Mayhem*

*Mobocracy*

*Montana*

*Night's Redemption*

*Manhunt*

*Merciless*

**The Last Message Trilogy**

*The Last Message*

*The Silent Protocol*

*The Final Cipher*

**L.A. Cyber Noir Mysteries**

*The Rose Slayer*

*Dark Web*

**Standalones**

*Operation George: A Gripping True Crime Story of an Audacious Undercover Sting*

*Comfort Zone: A Tale of Suspense*

*Death Among Us: An Anthology of Murder Mystery Short Stories*

AS KJ CORNWALL

**The Middleclere Mysteries**

*Shadows Over Middleclere*

**The Jessie Harper Paranormal Cosy Mysteries**

*The Cat's Tale*

*Murder on the Ferry*

*Murder at the Vicarage*

*Khan's Christmas Capers*

*Murder at the Mansion*

*Khan's Clerkenwell Catnapping Caper*

*The Vanishing Lady*

# BEHIND CARTEL LINES

**How I infiltrated and brought down Britain's biggest drug networks**

## STEPHEN BENTLEY

EBURY
SPOTLIGHT

EBURY SPOTLIGHT

UK | USA | Canada | Ireland | Australia
India | New Zealand | South Africa

Ebury Spotlight is part of the Penguin Random House group of companies
whose addresses can be found at global.penguinrandomhouse.com

Penguin Random House UK
One Embassy Gardens, 8 Viaduct Gardens, London SW11 7BW

penguin.co.uk
global.penguinrandomhouse.com

First published by Ebury Spotlight in 2025

1

Copyright © Stephen Bentley 2025
The moral right of the author has been asserted.

Penguin Random House values and supports copyright. Copyright fuels creativity, encourages diverse voices, promotes freedom of expression and supports a vibrant culture. Thank you for purchasing an authorised edition of this book and for respecting intellectual property laws by not reproducing, scanning or distributing any part of it by any means without permission. You are supporting authors and enabling Penguin Random House to continue to publish books for everyone. No part of this book may be used or reproduced in any manner for the purpose of training artificial intelligence technologies or systems. In accordance with Article 4(3) of the DSM Directive 2019/790, Penguin Random House expressly reserves this work from the text and data mining exception.

Typeset by seagulls.net

Printed and bound in Great Britain by Clays Ltd, Elcograf S.p.A.

The authorised representative in the EEA is Penguin Random House Ireland, Morrison Chambers, 32 Nassau Street, Dublin D02 YH68.

A CIP catalogue record for this book is available from the British Library

ISBN 9781529148152

 Penguin Random House is committed to a sustainable future for our business, our readers and our planet. This book is made from Forest Stewardship Council® certified paper.

*To all members of the Operation Julie team, from DI 'Leapy'
Lee down, the detectives and support personnel, whom I had the
privilege of serving with. Every single one of you was diligent,
professional, and a credit to this historical, unique
and pioneering British undercover operation.*

*Thank you, Zabrina, for the patience and understanding
in giving me the time and 'space' to complete this memoir.
More importantly, for helping me become a better person.*

*In memory of Peter, my beloved brother, best friend and confidant.*

Who am I? At this point, I have no clue.

**ANGEL PLOETNER**

## CONTENTS

| | | |
|---|---|---|
| One | What Was Operation Julie? | 1 |
| Two | Who Am I? | 4 |
| Three | LSD Culture | 18 |
| Four | Baby Detective | 24 |
| Five | LSD Culture Fast Learner | 31 |
| Six | Devizes and the Phoney War | 44 |
| Seven | Undercover Preparations | 57 |
| Eight | Llanddewi Brefi | 70 |
| Nine | Smiles | 76 |
| Ten | Blue | 83 |
| Eleven | Stones | 90 |
| Twelve | Movie Stars, Rock Stars | 96 |
| Thirteen | Internal Politics | 103 |
| Fourteen | Are You Guys Cops? | 108 |
| Fifteen | The Gun | 124 |
| Sixteen | Idiot! | 133 |
| Seventeen | Steve and Eric – Dealers | 144 |
| Eighteen | Doug | 152 |
| Nineteen | Chillum | 160 |
| Twenty | Christmas 1976 | 167 |
| Twenty-One | New Year | 177 |
| Twenty-Two | Cop Killer | 186 |

| Twenty-Three | No Way A Lab At Seymour Road | 193 |
| Twenty-Four | Old Acquaintances | 203 |
| Twenty-Five | Recall Papers | 212 |
| Twenty-Six | 124 Years' Jail | 220 |
| Twenty-Seven | 15 Pints | 229 |
| Twenty-Eight | Chief's Commendation | 238 |
| Twenty-Nine | House Arrest | 247 |
| Thirty | Resignation | 254 |
| Thirty-One | Unfinished Business | 261 |
| Thirty-Two | Lessons Learned | 273 |
| Thirty-Three | Duplicity | 286 |
| Thirty-Four | Smiles Revisited | 292 |
| Thirty-Five | Where Are They Now? | 297 |

Afterword............................................299

About the Author....................................301
Bibliography........................................303
Notes...............................................305

# ONE

# WHAT WAS OPERATION JULIE?

For many people, Operation Julie brings to mind a unique UK police investigation into the production of LSD by two drug rings during the mid-1970s. The investigation involved 11 police forces throughout England and Wales over a period of two-and-a-half years. It resulted in the break-up of one of the largest LSD manufacturing operations in the world. It culminated in 1977 with initial seizures of enough LSD to make 6.5 million tabs with a street value of £6.5 million. In today's money the drugs seized by the Julie squad is worth some £626 million.

*The Guinness World Book of Records* at one time showed these seizures as the world's largest by street value. As many as 120 people were arrested in the UK and France and over £800,000 was discovered in Swiss bank accounts worth over £5 million today.

In 1978, 15 defendants appeared at Bristol Crown Court. Most of the defendants pleaded guilty owing to the mass of incriminating evidence. Richard Kemp pleaded guilty and received 13 years in jail, as did Henry Todd. Nigel 'Leaf' Fielding and Alston Hughes 'Smiles' were sentenced to eight years. In total, the 15 defendants received a combined 124 years in jail.

As a result of the seizure, it was estimated the price of LSD tabs rose from £1 to £5 each, and that Operation Julie had removed 90 per cent of LSD from the British market. It is thought that LSD produced by the two labs had been exported to over 100 countries. In total, 1.1 million tabs and enough LSD crystal to make a further 6.5 million were discovered and destroyed.

The BBC[1] has said that Operation Julie began the era of the 'war on drugs', and I am unconvinced that the claim made in 2011 is correct. I do not believe any kind of war existed back then. That became obvious to any onlooker at the time who could see the bond that developed between many of the drugs gang members and the detectives involved in Operation Julie – in many cases forged out of mutual respect.

Although synonymous with LSD, Operation Julie also uncovered a huge plot to import vast quantities of cocaine into Britain. Two undercover cops unearthed that plot. This book tells of how detectives infiltrated the drugs gangs dealing in LSD. And, at the same time discovered the cocaine plot. I was one of those two detectives; the other was Eric Wright.

In writing this book I have had the invaluable assistance of the Llanddewi Brefi Log – the daily record of the undercover work performed by me and Eric Wright. I also relied on copies of witness statements I had recorded throughout the Operation Julie investigation. The memories of those days are still vivid but those documents filled in some key details.

A note for anyone unfamiliar with British legal jurisdictions, you may note references in my book to the entity of 'England and Wales' – it may assist you to know that the countries of England and Wales comprise a single legal jurisdiction. Scotland and Northern Ireland have their own legal systems. Thus, there are three discrete legal jurisdictions in the United Kingdom.

The book is neither pro nor anti drugs. Some people will always search for highs. I do not advocate the use of illegal drugs as I believe they are not necessary to live a meaningful life. Sometimes, they result in the opposite. And, on occasions, some end up with no life at all through drug abuse. I have no intention, nor wish, to preach to anyone.

I ask that you accept this book for what it is – an honest account of an ordinary man performing an extraordinary job. A job not many experience. I aim to help you understand what it is like to be an undercover detective – an infiltrator.

## TWO

# WHO AM I?

The Canadian could be an assassin. For sure, a big player dealing in vast quantities of heroin and cocaine. Bolivia is the source of the cocaine powder. It arrived into his control in an almost 100 per cent form. By the time it reached the streets of London it became a changed beast. If lucky, you may have had a purity of 45 per cent.

He did not control the chain of distribution all the way to street-level dealers. No need for that. Way too risky and more importantly, by the time he sold a one-pound 'weight' to me, Steve Jackson, he had made a handsome profit.

I am the British man talking to the Canadian in a Liverpool nightclub in 1976. Coke, charlie or snow, to use some of its names, remained the preserve of the wealthy back then. Expensive, but popular with rock stars. A massive market and a huge opportunity for profit existed in Britain.

The deal had been laid out on the table. The Canadian and I became parties to a conspiracy to import serious weights of cocaine into Britain.

The Canadian's mood changed. Why? Not clear to me at all. Without him revealing too many details, the Canadian had impressed me with the plan.

- ☑ Bolivia
- ☑ Go-fast boat in place
- ☑ Air hostess to bring the contraband into Britain
- ☑ Prices and discounts for quantity

Snap! The mood did change, and how!

'Are you guys cops?'

Wham! This question hit me like a vivid lightning strike from a clear blue sky. The words rolled around inside my head like rolling thunder.

A simulated assassination followed. A double-tap from a silenced semi-automatic pistol favoured by professional hitmen the world over. A close-range execution.

He raised one hand next to my head. The Canadian pointed his joined forefinger and middle finger, imitating a gun. The fingertips touched my skin.

He silently mouthed the silenced spitting sound as two imaginary shells splattered my brains out of the gaping exit wounds at the far side of my head.

*Pop. Pop.*

• • •

From 1976 to 1980 Steve Bentley the detective turned into Steve Jackson the drug dealer, who turned back into Steve Bentley, the police officer. I am both men and this is my story.

Before you follow me on my story's journey, this may be as good a time as any to answer a question asked of me over the years. The pity is it was never asked by those who influenced my career and the remainder of my life. The question? 'What goes on inside an undercover cop's head?' Permit me to elaborate with the benefit of hindsight.

Life is full of uncertainty when you work deep undercover. Who is she? Who is he? Is she a bad guy? Is he a bad guy? If so, are they capable of harming me, capable of violence?

There are always more questions than answers. Who am I? Are you two people or does one take over from the other? It's an enigma. I don't know the answer but I know it fascinates some people. They have told me as much.

Where am I? Some venues are more comfortable than others. Some places I could sense it was possible to relax, but only to a degree. Other places I had to be constantly mentally vigilant. Then you must deal with substances that mess with your head. Alcohol and cannabis all change one's perceptions of reality. Have you ever been so drunk or stoned you end up fearful of making some big *faux pas*, like telling the boss to fuck off? Chances are you have, or at least most of us have. Now think of that feeling. Multiply it by one thousand. It gives you an inkling of the sheer willpower needed to concentrate while undercover to avoid slip-ups.

The truth is I could never allow a conflict to take place in my head whether sober or not. I had to forget Steve Bentley and become totally immersed in the psyche of Steve Jackson. I could not afford a slip-up. My life may have been in danger.

My values were torn up and new values substituted. I was ready to do almost anything to further my cover. I guess the checks and balances in the system made me toe the line. Eric was a key factor in me not overstepping the mark. My brain worked on schemes and plans. Eric would never have countenanced them. I could have gone deeper undercover, losing myself in this other identity. I couldn't do it with my 'watchdog' constantly by my side. Just as well, I may have gone 'somewhere' and done something drastic.

Eric by all accounts was not my intended partner. Dick Lee, the Operation Julie commander, had someone else earmarked for the role. Again, by all accounts, it was a good thing Eric replaced him. The original choice was more hippie than any real hippie and has probably smoked more hash than has ever been grown in, say, Afghanistan. We may have led each other astray.

Eric was a welcome constraint, a valuable ally preventing me from indulging in too many flights of fantasy. Eric was solid of character and by his own admission, didn't think too much. He had simple tastes and straightforward values. I was more complicated. I was a gambler, a chancer, impulsive and excited by the danger. Life undercover was one great adrenaline rush fuelled by copious amounts of alcohol, hash, weed and some cocaine. I was off the leash. I was also a thinker. Always trying to stay one step ahead of the game – *What if this? What if that?* It was the way I functioned. It was a normal process for me. And I was a good liar, most times basing the lie on a kernel of truth. Perhaps the easiest example is the retention of my Liverpool roots while posing as Steve Jackson.

It was freedom. I was free to do as I pleased, when I pleased, and with whom I pleased. I could be intimate with anyone who wanted the same, break laws, fight and do drugs. I revelled in music I would not have been exposed to. A culture that would have evaded me – the Steve Bentley me. It was exhilarating! It was a high much higher than all the other highs.

I dressed and talked and walked differently. The suits, shirts and ties of the conventional detective were consigned to mothballs in the wardrobe. Old worn-out sneakers, torn jeans, a denim shirt and jacket were my uniform. Long hair and a beard gave me the wild look. There was a wild look in my eyes too, as the booze and drugs began to take effect on my appearance. 'Don't fuck with me' was a look I perfected when the occasion warranted it. Otherwise, I was the likeable, affable conversationalist who got on with all and sundry, locals, non-locals, dealers and non-dealers, drug users and straight people.

The hardest part of going deep undercover was returning home. I was reluctant to do so. I had put Steve Bentley out of mind. To go home to a wife who only knew Steve Bentley was tough. Most of that time I was there in body only. My head was elsewhere. I wished away the minutes and the hours until it was time to return. There was a sigh of welcome relief on walking out of my front door, turning the key in my car and driving off towards Eric and Wales. *Free again! Fuck the bills and the routine ... fuck everything to do with married life.* That state of mind continued for so many years.

I was at my most vulnerable during the drive to Eric's in my car. It didn't have a ghost plate. In retrospect that was a mistake. Anyone could have seen me in my own car. A phone call to a bent copper would have revealed who I really was. Inwardly, I must have been conscious of this as I only relaxed after parking my car and jumping into the van with Eric by my side.

It helped we didn't talk much about 'the job' – police work, or other police officers. Eric wasn't a gossip and it was one of the things I liked about him. We both had the ability to chat about all sorts of issues, both mundane and out of the ordinary. We were 'normal,' whatever that is. Sure, on the way to Wales we talked about Smiles, our target in the distribution chain, but he wasn't the main topic of conversation.

In retrospect, playing it cool with Smiles worked to our benefit. Like a girl you are keen on – play it cool and see if she comes running. Smiles didn't exactly come running. Yet, I am sure our stand-off approach helped allay his suspicions about us. It helped there was no expectation of Smiles wanting to deal in LSD with us. We were infiltrators and intelligence gatherers. We weren't expected to do deals with Smiles. That idea was discounted from day one.

## TWO

Permit me take you to the immediate aftermath of my undercover days before we embark on the journey through the earlier years leading up to Operation Julie. Then, once you know me better, I will tell you my story.

...

Depression is no fun. My superiors had beckoned, no, ordered me to attend Hampshire Police Headquarters in Winchester in the March of 1980.

I drove myself to Winchester from Farnborough. It seemed a long 20 miles. The radio turned off in the car. No cassette in the slot. The only noise inside my own head. A spinning noise. But silent. More like a whirring noise. But silent. Noise can be silent. I had no idea what I was doing save for the fact I had an appointment with the police force doctor and the Deputy Chief Constable (DCC). The DCC is like an Assistant Commissioner of Police in the United States.

In a state of fugue, I managed to walk through the entrance doors of the multi-storey police headquarters. I introduced myself to Reception by showing my warrant card. She, the receptionist, expected me and told me to take the lift to the higher reaches of the building. There, a seat awaited me. I also waited for the summons by one of the gods. It felt like a flashback to schooldays and being sent to see the beak. Like a good boy, I complied and waited.

The route to the floor of the gods seemed littered with the faces of people familiar to me. Some of them were unfamiliar, but they appeared to know me. On occasions, someone said hello. A sort of nervous twitch hello, not a 'how the hell are you' kind of hello. I was aware but unaware. It seemed like a void. Kind of like watching a silent movie but with me as one of the actors.

I had a two o'clock appointment. A good time owing to the fact my recent habits included lying in bed until at least noon. I sat on a chair in a corridor and waited. I stared at the floor, stared at the walls and stared at the ceiling. No windows to stare out. I waited and stared. Silent whirring noises still spun in my head. My thoughts were a blank canvas with splashes of invisible colour. *Is this real? Am I dreaming it?* My thoughts would not leave my head.

'Sergeant Bentley?' A woman in a nurse's uniform startled me.

'Yes.'

'Please come in.'

She gestured towards a door with a sign: Force Surgeon.

Glancing at my watch, I saw the hands had reached three o'clock. I recall thinking, *I have been waiting here since 1.45pm!*

The doctor introduced himself. He made a point of telling me his speciality – a general practitioner. Not a psychiatrist or psychologist.

He started with, 'So what's the problem?'

'I don't know. You tell me.'

'You have been off work sick for some three months now. Is that correct?'

## TWO

'Yeah.'

'When do you plan on returning?'

'Straight after this meeting.'

'Oh! Good.'

'Yeah, I'm going straight home after this meeting.'

'I see. I thought you …'

'I know what you thought I meant.'

'So, what about a return to work?'

'I have no idea.'

'Hmm. Okay, tell me how you feel.'

'Like shit.'

'Please be more explicit.'

'Like fucking shit. How's that for explicit?'

My nothing in my head would not allow me to be explicit. I could not explain what was troubling me. I knew what it felt like but it was in a deep part of me that I could not see or touch. I knew it was there. It had a rawness like an open wound. In place of frankness that I found impossible, I asked a question.

'Is this confidential? Between me and you. Doctor and patient stuff.'

'Well, I have a duty to make a report on your fitness to work.'

The word 'well' at the beginning of an answer usually bodes ill in my experience. It is like the use of 'with respect' when addressing a matter with which you do not agree.

'Look, with respect, how can you make a report when you're not qualified?'

'Excuse me ...'

'You heard; you aren't qualified. Can you see anything physically wrong with me?'

'No.'

'Well, there you are then. I'm off!'

The corridor and the chair welcomed me back. They didn't wish to talk and I didn't need to explain anything to them. I waited for the summons into the DCC's office. His secretary spoke to me after I had been waiting for an hour. It is now 4.30pm. She apologised to me, telling me the DCC had been unexpectedly involved in a long but important telephone call.

'Okay, thanks.' But I wasn't thinking *Okay* at all.

*Important? What's more important than keeping an appointment with me? This is my future up for discussion.* My thoughts were still whirring. *DCC?* He was known for his sourpuss face and hard man reputation. The DCC role in all police forces is known as an arbiter of internal disciplinary matters. The thought train continued ... *Maybe heads are going to roll?*

I swear I saw disembodied heads rolling along the corridor. I laughed out loud. *I'm for the high jump?* popped my next thought. *Perhaps Fosbury[2] flopping would be a good way to enter the DCC's office?* These thoughts ran through my mind at the same time as I clearly heard Procol Harum's 'A Whiter Shade of Pale.'

## TWO

At that point, a lucidity returned. It became so clear what I had to do. I rose from the silent chair, walked to the lift and retraced my journey to the floor of the gods in reverse. I knew I had made my decision. Fuck them all!

No one in the history of the Hampshire Police had dared to walk out of such an appointment before or since that day.

I was asked to be explicit. This is explicit. I had not worked for three months prior to my appointment with the DCC. I had reported sick. I had seen my own doctor who confirmed depression. My doctor referred my case to a local hospital for me to see a psychiatrist. I failed to attend the appointments.

Depression is no longer a stigma like it was in the 1980s. I could not countenance that I needed help. My pride and stubbornness meant I was too ashamed to admit I was no longer in control.

What caused my depression?

In 1980, I, Steve Bentley, believed I was a career police officer. I was proud of what I had achieved in my undercover role during Operation Julie. It was the high point of my police career and a memory I will carry with me to the grave. I fought and worked hard to get to a point to be handpicked by Dick Lee for Operation Julie in 1976. I clawed my way there and never wanted Julie to end. The Julie squad evolved into a formidable group of investigators and ought to have been allowed to continue, particularly to combat the gangs importing cocaine and heroin into Britain.

My own undercover role as Steve Jackson had a price. I became alcohol dependent and, to a lesser degree, dependent upon cannabis and cocaine. It proved disastrous for my second marriage, which dissolved shortly after the conclusion of Operation Julie.

A promotion came my way following Operation Julie. I became a Detective Sergeant based in Farnborough, Hampshire. I flew by the seat of my pants in that role. The job was all too easy and so mundane following my undercover exploits. I arrived late for work too many times, caused by hangovers from the previous night's drinking. I also met my future third wife. She, or rather my relationship with her, was the catalyst for my slump into a deep depression.

When I met her I was drinking heavily, crazily. Stopping out all night, often falling into a drunken stupor in a pub. I was also still smoking dope.

It was love between Catherine and me. The longest, closest, most passionate and spiritual relationship I had encountered. I moved in with her while still married to my second wife and still a Detective Sergeant in Farnborough.

What followed is possibly scarcely believable now in the twenty-first century. I became a victim of an attitude so typical of the police force in the late 1970s and early 1980s. My superiors objected to me living with a woman while unmarried. This objection took the form of transferring me to Southampton, 40 miles away from Farnborough. To rub salt into the wound, they expected me to perform uniformed duties as a Sergeant and allocated me a single man's hostel to live in.

This was unacceptable on many fronts.

I was a detective through and through; from the tender age of twenty-one, I had been recognised as a good thief-taker. My high scoring in the final tests of the Home Office Detective Training Course had got me noticed. Following my move from Merseyside to Hampshire in 1971, I spent some time back in uniform. I detested that time. I worked hard and earned my right to shed the uniform. It did not come easy.

Now, I saw myself faced with a blatant effort to separate me from Catherine and a forced move back to uniform duties. I could not countenance either prospect. I was seriously depressed by these developments. The mess was exacerbated by a visit from Norman Green, a police Superintendent who knew me well and held me in high regard.

Green came to Catherine's home in Farnborough and asked to speak with me privately. That seemed fine by me, but Catherine sharply told Green that anything he had to say could be said in front of her. She remained.

My absence from work came to be treated as a disappearance. I failed to communicate with anyone about my sickness. I simply stopped going to work. My disappearance began to be treated with some urgency when an all-force bulletin circulated to locate me.

No one could find me except Green. He made no headway in his attempts to persuade me to go back to work and accept my transfer to Southampton. He made no headway because telling me what to do without listening reinforced my stubbornness. Perhaps if he had asked me to explain and pour out my troubles, we may have made progress. But I doubt it. I did not want to talk about work or the R-word – responsibility.

I found it galling that he reported back that I had been found living in squalor. Nothing could have been further from the truth. Catherine was a homemaker. Okay, when he visited, the house may have been a tad untidy. Her four kids lived there, and Catherine worked nights at the local hospital so maybe she was busy the day Mr Green visited and failed to tidy up. I am sure that Catherine would also appreciate me mentioning that this visit took place without warning.

Of course, an impression gained momentum about my craziness, no doubt given further impetus by me living with a woman with four kids. Friends were concerned about me. Some even thought of me as reckless.

These were superiors who had no idea about undercover work, drugs, alcohol abuse, or an assassination threat in Liverpool by a Canadian cocaine dealer. Green and the others expected me to shake off depression like a stray piece of cotton on my clothing. Just brush it off and get on with things, report back for duty in Southampton.

Ex-Detective Sergeant 410, Stephen Bentley, reporting for duty! How could I report for duty in the middle of a nervous breakdown? It took me many years to realise that in 1980 I suffered from more than acute depression.

Let me say at the outset that I do not seek sympathy, nor do I regret the events that took place between 1976 and 1980. I simply wish to tell my story.

# THREE

# LSD CULTURE

Operation Julie has often been referred to as a police undercover operation. Nothing could be further from the truth. A lot of the investigation required good old-fashioned routine detective work. Much of it involved surveillance of targets and suspects. The 25 members of the Operation Julie team tracking or tailing the suspects' vehicles carried out this surveillance work. Surveillance was not limited to tailing suspects, but also homes and business premises for lengthy periods. The Operation Julie detectives even posed as innocent holidaymakers and, on one occasion, as surveyors. All done to disguise the fact they were watchers.

None of this is true undercover work.

When you go undercover you assume a completely new identity. You mix with and hope to infiltrate the bad guys. 'Infiltrator' is a better description of deep undercover work. It is not working as a narco (narcotics officer) or a police officer masquerading as a drug buyer. He or she invariably gets to go home at night, works a shift and returns to normality. They carry a badge and retain their identity. Infiltration is a stressful and demanding role. It can last for days, hours, weeks, months or even years.

Only four true undercover officers worked on Operation Julie. Eric Wright and myself were two of them. The other two, Martyn Pritchard and Andy Beaumont, drifted in and out. They did not spend days, weeks and months undercover, constantly pretending to be someone else. Imagine living eight months of your life existing as another person.

So many myths have surrounded Operation Julie. Part of that myth-building has been caused by lazy journalism over the years, which continues today. The year 2016 was the fortieth anniversary of the formation of the Operation Julie squad. News articles appeared harking back to the UK's biggest ever drugs bust. Lazy journalism is still repeated even now.

Storylines and headlines such as 'Julie's 'hippies' put Richard Kemp's Tregaron home under surveillance and noted his regular 50-mile commutes to Plas Llysyn, an old mansion in Carno near Llanidloes.'[3] And from the same BBC source, '… another group of 'hippies' monitored the mansion from an old caravan, and when they secretly broke in, water samples taken from the cellar chemically matched LSD samples the police had previously seized.' The same BBC article spoke of '… dozens of undercover officers who were sent into west Wales posing as hippies to place them under surveillance during a 13-month operation.'

Those BBC statements are inaccurate. I repeat – only four true undercover officers worked on Operation Julie. Eric Wright and I were two of them.

# THREE

What follows is a true story. It does not pretend to be the whole story of Operation Julie as that is well documented elsewhere. Operation Julie, rightly so, is associated with breaking up one of the largest LSD manufacturing facilities and worldwide distribution networks the world has ever seen.

What is not known is the detail of how my undercover work, with my undercover partner Eric, connected into a huge plot to import cocaine into Britain and identified the main players in that conspiracy. It is a personal narrative where I hope to show you at least a glimpse into undercover police work. I will do what I never allowed during my undercover days – I will let you into my head.

As for the conspirators in the Operation Julie saga, they knew the risks in manufacturing and distributing a Class A drug. One of the main characters in my story, Smiles, summed that up so succinctly to me. I wanted to meet him following the arrests and I did so in a police cell at Swindon Police Station.

He kindly said to me, 'No hard feelings. It's all part of the game.'

The advocates of the use of LSD are articulate and intelligent people. However, may I remind them of what Aldous Huxley himself thought about the use of LSD and I quote Tendler and May[4]:

*From the very beginning there had been an edge in the drug experiences bordering, frighteningly, on insanity. Huxley's second wife, Laura, herself an LSD psychotherapist, later wrote: 'Always Aldous emphasizes how delicately and respectfully these chemicals should be used.' LSD should only be taken with a doctor's consent and then when the subject was peaceful, in good health, friendly surroundings and wise company.*

Some of the main players in the conspiracy held the view that they were entitled to 'spread the word' about LSD in a similar vein to Timothy Leary and others involved in the earliest days of the LSD counterculture. If they were as intelligent as many, including me, make out, then it is astounding they engaged in both self-deception and hypocrisy on a grand scale.

Smiles knew he was a dealer. He lived by his wits and selling drugs — nothing more and nothing less. He was honest to himself. Kemp was the chemist manufacturing LSD, with Christine Bott as his willing assistant. The American, David Solomon, with connections back to the Brotherhood of Eternal Love, recruited Kemp to make acid. The pseudo-altruistic messages pouring forth from the likes of Kemp and Bott were just poppycock. Money motivated them also. They just found it inconvenient to admit it. Okay, they lived the simple life in the Welsh cottage with the goats and the vegetable patch. But how many 'good lifers' like them also had Swiss bank accounts? Furthermore, if the account by Tendler and May is correct, then why did Kemp become so concerned with money in his early days in France working as the chemist for Solomon?

The original LSD culture centred around the beat generation of the 1950s and early 1960s. The drug was initially the preserve of artists, authors and academia. Eventually, even the early 'evangelists' of LSD, treating it as a kind of sacred object, succumbed to the temptation to make easy money. The Brotherhood of Eternal Love is a story heavily featuring the criminal Hell's Angels gangs of California. Operation Julie and the massive drugs ring it smashed is a legacy of those days.

All the proselytising falling from the mouths of the advocates of LSD also conveniently forgets another factor. Polydrug use is commonplace. Most street dealers and users of drugs sell or use more than just one single type of drug. This opens opportunities for the drug user who is new to the scene of being attracted to the prospect of trying and experimenting with new drugs. Smiles had access to LSD, cocaine and cannabis. In my experience, both as a former undercover officer, drugs squad detective and criminal defence barrister, that is common.

I appreciate that the following tales are apocryphal, but they are true. A neighbour of mine told me many years ago he still suffered unpleasant flashbacks years after he ceased to use LSD. Turning to the topic of cannabis, a close friend told me he had stopped using cannabis on a regular basis. Why? He had reached a stage when he forgot important things to do and important appointments in his work diary.

The responsible advice to anyone who wishes to trip on acid is to have a 'sitter' and ensure you are in a peaceful and comfortable state of mind. Unfortunately, it is not everyone who follows that advice. It isn't like your acid tab comes with a health warning and usage instructions in a container like you get from a pharmacy with a prescription or over-the-counter drug.

The effects of any hallucinogenic drug, including cannabis, can be unpredictable. You can Google your own sources, if you so wish, to find out more about 'bad acid trips' but I did find one after a cursory search[5]. Surely, the unpredictability is good enough reason for the likes of LSD and cannabis to be outlawed? If you hold the opinion cannabis is not a hallucinogenic, think again.

I don't believe I am a hypocrite. I used drugs during my undercover days and since then on several occasions. I haven't used any for years now. I am open-minded about certain drugs. I neither advocate their use nor condemn anyone that uses them. I recognised the dangers of drug use in my own life and what I object to are the one-sided arguments used in the debate about drugs.

In case you wonder, and it isn't a spoiler, I never did a trip on acid. It was never a problem to refuse acid. Acidheads and the 'head world' in general know it's not for everyone. Even if it is for you, there is a universal acceptance in the drug world that you must be 'in the moment' to contemplate dropping even a single tab.

**FOUR**

# BABY DETECTIVE

The Operation Julie squad was formed in 1976. Early in that year, I was a detective assigned to the Hampshire Drugs Squad. It was an unfamiliar role for me. I had been a real detective in the Lancashire police force from 1968 to 1972, based in Merseyside. Working on major crime throughout the old county of Lancashire and the new county of Merseyside.

I was a product of the 1960s. The only drugs I knew of as a teenager in Liverpool were purple hearts (amphetamine pills). And, that you could buy reefers (joints) in Liverpool 8. Drugs back then were available through the West Indian community. To be precise, in the *shebeens* (illegal drinking clubs) of Toxteth. Weed was available there. As a young police officer at the back end of the 1960s, I became aware of heroin addicts because of a spate of chemist shop burglaries committed by heroin addicts.

Most of my probationary police service happened in Eccles, Greater Manchester. I soon transferred to Kirkby, a large Liverpool overspill town. My probationary period ended in 1968. Eccles is where I first developed my hankering to become a detective. One memorable episode drew me toward the Criminal Investigation Department (CID).

As I walked my beat, I started to chat to a guy working on a car in the street. I wore a full uniform.

I wished him, 'Good day!'

He was under the car bonnet and popped his head out, smiled and said, 'How are you, officer?'

He was a little older than me, perhaps he was 25.

'Your car?' I asked.

'Yes, just checking an oil leak. Do you fancy a brew?'

'Good idea. I've still got three hours to kill of this shift. I'd love a cup of tea, milk, no sugar please.'

His car was parked outside of his terraced house. A few minutes later he reappeared from the house with two mugs of tea in his oily hands.

'There you go, constable. Enjoy.'

We stood in the street chatting and drinking our tea.

'Fancy a smoke?' He offered me a cigarette from an opened pack.

'Yeah, thanks.' I loosened the chin strap and removed my helmet to light up. It's strange how that seemed to make it okay to smoke in uniform in public.

The conversation was about cars. I spotted a new-looking car stereo fitted in the dashboard of this car. It appeared younger than the car. The chat turned to car radios and stereos.

'You got a car, officer?'

'No, not yet but I'm saving for one.'

'Shame,' he said, 'I can get you whatever car radio you want.'

'How's that?'

'I pinch them.'

'Yeah, pull the other one.'

'No, I'm serious officer. I nick 'em from parked cars. I can get you what you want. Just tell me and I'll get it.'

It remains a mystery to me why he started to confess to a series of thefts. For two years he had been stealing car radios from parked cars. I arrested him.

On arrival at the police station, the Sergeant told me to take my prisoner upstairs to the CID office. That inner sanctum which was invitation-only. You didn't go there unless told. A detective known as Big John took on the case after I told him what had happened. He asked if I wanted to stick around and see how the 'real police' work. I did. I was in awe.

Shortly after that incident, a house burglar murdered an elderly lady in Eccles. A small army of strangers took over the police station. It became populated by a squad of detectives drawn from all over Lancashire. Again, I was in awe. These guys oozed confidence. I sat in silence during the refreshment break in the police canteen. I listened to the 'war stories' and jokes, soaking up the atmosphere.

Discretion is important in policing. I learned about it in Eccles. I saw a young boy stealing bottles of milk from doorsteps. I followed him to a nearby house. He entered clutching about six bottles under his arms. I decided to knock on the door. This took place in the early hours.

A big tough-looking guy opened the door. He appeared to be about 35. His black hair was swept back with grease and he was wearing braces to hold up his trousers. In an unmistakable Cockney accent, he asked me what I wanted. A direct question but polite in his tone. I told him what I had seen.

'Come in, come in officer. I'm sure we can sort this out.'

I walked into the death throes of a party. Bottles and cans of booze littered the room. A blonde Barbara Windsor lookalike smiled and said hello. About ten people filled the room.

'Now look, if it's about the milk ...' the big guy had a fiver in his hand. He thrust it toward me.

'No thanks,' I said.

'Well, have a drink then.'

I had a can of beer with them and admonished the kid who had stolen the milk. Everyone smiled. I later found out that it was one of the Krays I had been speaking to.

I refused money from one of the Krays (two 1960s East London gangster brothers, Ronnie and Reggie). I never took a penny off anyone in the whole of my police career. I saw corruption. I saw a uniformed police constable steal a chocolate bar from a shop. I went to the shop after the alarm had been set off. The shop owner saw him too. Dismissal from the police service for that officer was a correct decision. In my early CID days, I also saw corruption. The instances were few and far between, but they did happen.

One such incident started off as humorous. I had started an investigation into a break-in at a men's fashion shop in

Crosby, Liverpool. Thieves cleared it out of suits, shirts and shoes. An informant led us to a block of 13-storey flats in nearby Litherland. I had a search warrant to search four of the flats on the ninth and tenth floors.

As we climbed out of our vehicles, we heard shouts, 'Bizzies! Bizzies are here.' Bizzies is Liverpool slang for police. On looking up toward the flats it seemed like it was raining. Not cats and dogs, but coats, suits, trousers and shoes, all still wrapped in their plastic protection – a funny sight. There seemed no point in searching. The stolen goods and the evidence now scattered over the car park.

The evidence ended up in the back of a police van. Thousands of pounds' worth of stolen clothes filled it. One uniform officer was stood at the back of the van loading the goods. We then drove to Seaforth Police Station to deposit the goods in the property store, the same officer now responsible for unloading the van.

As he passed each item over to waiting officers, he said, 'One for the store and one for the boys.'

I walked away. Whistleblowers were not in vogue in those days.

I developed a reputation among my fellow detectives. Don't do anything underhand in front of Steve Bentley. He will not play ball. A good example of this was a search carried out by me and two of my former colleagues. A terrified young boy of about 17 had finally gathered the courage to report a serious crime. He had been a shop assistant in a stand-alone kiosk part of the larger main store, selling liquor, beer and cigarettes.

For six months, a small group of men terrorised him. They would enter his kiosk when he was alone and demand bottles of liquor and cigarettes. At first, he declined but later succumbed to threats. One of those threats involved squirting lighter fluid over his head from a toy gun – a water pistol. The gang then lit a match and threatened to set him on fire. He described the water pistol as yellow in colour.

We obtained a search warrant. I set off to search the ringleader's home. I travelled there with my Detective Sergeant (DS) and another detective. Under instructions, I walked into the living room to search there alone. The DS and the other detective marched straight to the bedroom.

Within seconds of entering the bedroom, I heard my DS exclaim, 'Oh! Look at what I have found.' The tone of voice and the gestures straight out of ham-acting school.

He had a yellow plastic water pistol in his hands when I poked my head in through the bedroom door. It felt wrong. I knew it was wrong but had no proof.

The ringleader in the strongest terms protested his innocence saying, 'It's a plant. You bastards have fitted me up.'

He maintained that stance all the way through to trial. I gave evidence from the witness box for three days, cross-examined by counsel for all five accused on the search. What could I say? I told the truth. What I thought was pure conjecture on my part. Thoughts and conjecture are invariably inadmissible in a court of law. The DS was cunning enough to send me into that room alone. I wasn't privy to what did happen during the search of that bedroom.

After Eccles, my transfer to Kirkby took place. Plenty of opportunities there to make arrests for crime. Newtown in the popular 1960s BBC police drama series *Z Cars* was Kirkby. I got to meet several of the actors when they visited Kirkby. They came to gain some first-hand experience of real policing. In no time at all I was performing temporary CID duties at the tender age of 21. When selected to attend the Home Office Detective Training Course, I reacted with delight. My career as a detective now underway, a baby detective. I had a lot to learn but I learned fast.

Before that detective career started, I learned a lot about people from my time in uniform in Kirkby. It was a tough place. Boarding up the local shops the norm back then, even when they were open during the day. Crime, violence and drunkenness were rife. The town had a reputation of notoriety. A bit of an unfair assessment, as many honest, law-abiding families lived there. But to most people Kirkby had a 'wild west' reputation. It was somewhere you played tick (tag) with hatchets. Yet, I felt comfortable and at home in Kirkby.

# FIVE

# FAST LEARNER

Kirkby was similar in many ways to Huyton where I lived as a kid. The two Merseyside suburbs are divided by the East Lancashire Road and separated by about five miles. Both are predominantly working class, so that was another reason for my feeling at home in Kirkby. Like Huyton, Kirkby is full of characters all too ready to spin a yarn with typical Scouse[6] wit and humour. Both towns also had a reputation for violence. Sometimes the humour was used to distract from the violence. For example, an area of Huyton – a vast housing estate known as Woolfall Heath, was better known as 'Mau-Mau[7] territory' by local people. It was a location viewed as a no-go area by outsiders and rent collectors.

Kirkby was home to many hard men. Andy was a great bear of a man. He had a shaven head and was proud of the many scars criss-crossing his skull – all marks left by the many police batons that had cracked down on it. It would take several officers to subdue and arrest him when he was full of ale and in a fighting mood.

The town was also home to a large family I got to know quite well. One of the older sons became a successful professional boxer. But some of his brothers chose a life of crime, much to the despair of their mother. She was a lovely gentle woman married to a former seaman who hailed from West Africa. One of her younger sons enjoyed taking high-powered cars for a spin. The only problem was the cars didn't belong to him nor did he have a licence to drive. I followed him in a high-speed chase at night trying to catch up with him. He drove too fast for me. He was a fast driver, but dangerous too. I decided enough was enough once he went through the red light on the busy East Lancashire Road junction. Anyway, I recognised him and would arrest him later. I did arrest him.

The youngster appeared at a Liverpool court. Waiting all day for the case to be called on, I chatted to both his parents for hours. Mum pleaded with me to say a good word for her boy. I did but only because I believed in my testimonial. Mum and Dad expressed their gratitude because all three of us believed my words saved the boy serving a custodial sentence. I know their gratitude was genuine. They were good people.

The Kirkby police also had some hard men. One of them a most genial, boyish, inoffensive-looking man from Belfast. Yet looks can be deceptive. He had been a good welterweight boxer in Northern Ireland before joining the Lancashire police. The word was he had won ABA titles. My night shift responded to a disturbance late one night. Neighbours had complained about the racket from one of the adjoining flats. On our arrival, we found a man stripped to the waist. He wanted to fight anyone and everyone. He hurled milk bottles from the balcony towards us, the uniformed police.

He was also chucking them at the onlookers on the car park. Everybody was in danger.

After quite a struggle and his eventual arrest, we took him to Kirkby Police Station. He continued wanting to fight and refused to enter his cell. The Belfast man, as I will call him, stripped off to the waist and invited the detainee to fulfil his desire to fight. The maniac detainee, that is an apt description, wanted an assurance that it would be a fair fight with no interventions. He received that assurance.

A flurry of straight left jabs to the maniac's face rocked him back. His face soon turned to a mask of blood and snot. The maniac gave up, raising his hands in surrender. Several buckets of water sluiced the blood from his face and he meekly entered his cell. The next day he appeared at court with a swollen, bruised face.

When asked by the magistrates' clerk what had happened, the maniac said, 'Nothing, sir. Nothing at all. I'm guilty.'

Most of these hard men were like that. If beaten fairly and squarely, there would be no complaint about heavy-handed police officers.

These Kirkby uniform days confirmed my ambition to be a detective. One incident stands out in my mind. I attended the scene of a road traffic accident early in the morning. A little girl had run out in front of a bus and was fatally injured.

I arrived on the scene to witness the still figure of the girl laying on the road. A pretty little girl and still wearing her floral-patterned school uniform. Her hair neatly tied back, no doubt by her mother, only a short time ago. Her legs had been broken in the impact. But the sight of the blood flowing from underneath her head turned my stomach.

I decided I was ill-equipped to be a first responder at the scene of traffic accidents. Dead bodies on morgue tables never bothered me. Dead little girls who, moments earlier, were happily running around, were another matter.

My permanent CID posting arrived. It came within weeks of passing the nine-week Home Office Detective Training course. Kirkby was my first CID posting. After Kirkby, I worked in the CID office at Crosby on the banks of the River Mersey. Crosby was a complete contrast to Kirkby. From Crosby Police Station, we investigated crime in wealthy suburbs like Blundellsands and Hightown. I soon learned how to deal with a different class of people. They weren't the working class that I belonged to and I had to adapt. Some of the adaptations were easier than others. I was young and naïve and had a lot to learn about human behaviour and sexual peccadilloes. My DS at Crosby was a fine detective. Like many of that era, he had a penchant for drinking. Every night was a booze excursion to a different pub. He was well known in all of them.

This DS was particularly fond of one pub in one of the wealthier parts of the patch and I soon found out the reason. There was a banker and his attractive wife who were regulars in that pub. They had a routine of inviting my DS and his detectives back to their substantial home after the pub had closed. That is what happened on my first trip to this pub with my DS. I had my eyes opened after we arrived at the banker's home. The invitation was not restricted to having a few drinks. No, for my DS it was more than that. The banker ushered his wife and the DS into the front living room. I made to follow.

'No, stay in the hall. We'll have a drink here and I'll get my gun,' the banker said.

I was curious. He returned from the kitchen with glasses, a bottle of single malt and an air rifle!

He set up a dartboard at the far end of the 40-yard hall.

'Okay, you go first,' he said as he handed me the air rifle.

We had target practice, drank the fine malt whisky and listened to my DS humping the wife in the room next door.

'Fuck me! Fuck me harder!'

The banker masturbated on hearing his wife. I was on a steep learning curve about people and human nature.

Within twelve months of my first CID posting, I joined the elite Lancashire Task Force. This was a mobile squad of detectives, a bit like London's Flying Squad without the corruption. I soon investigated some six murders throughout the county. All within a twelve-month time scale. This was real police, as they would say in *The Wire*[8]. It was a fantastic experience and a great grounding for a young detective like me.

The Task Force was Joe Mounsey's idea. Sometimes the local CID did not have enough manpower. Our purpose was to help the local CID whenever a serious crime took place. It required a concentrated effort to solve the crime quickly. He was present to give the morning and evening briefing and debrief every single day. Mr Mounsey was a great detective and it was a pleasure to serve under him. He treated us like men. He expected us to perform and we did, partly because of the high regard for him as a man and a detective. We had a further bonus: new cars to drive, two-litre Ford Cortinas. They had no outward police markings but were fitted with VHF radio sets, a pop-up POLICE/STOP sign in the rear window, sirens and a magnetic blue lamp capable of roof mounting.

I almost failed the selection process for this elite squad. The interview took place at Knowsley Hall near Liverpool, the home of Lord Derby. The main hall is accessible via a long gravel drive. It must be about two miles long. On my way in for the interview, I thought back to the days when I used to deliver newspapers there as a boy living in Huyton. It was a long haul down that drive in a car on the day of my interview. Yet, it didn't seem so long pushing the pedals of my bicycle to deliver the Sunday papers. The South West Lancashire CID Task Force had taken over part of the main hall as temporary HQ. It helped the Derby family pay for the enormous bills involved in the upkeep of their ancestral home. At least it did until they set up the Knowsley Zoo and Wildlife Park in the grounds.

The library served as the interview venue. It was a huge room with bookshelves that started at floor level and stopped at the ceiling. I caught sight of one of those sliding librarian's ladders in the corner of my eye. The room had a massive oak table in the middle. Joe Mounsey and other senior detectives interviewed me. I thought the process had gone well until I stood up to leave the room. Retracing my steps towards the exit, all I could see were bookshelves and books. Panic set in. Fumbling about, I found there was a sliding panel door. From the inside, it resembled another bookshelf. With a sigh of relief, I slid the door open.

I heard Joe Mounsey call out, 'Well done, lad. You passed the final test.'

My chest puffed out. I was in and out. In the squad and out of the library.

• • •

On moving to Hampshire, I missed this real police work. I say 'real' because my early days on the drugs squad did not impress me. The brief involved dealing with street-level dealers and kids for simple possession of a small amount of cannabis. They had their own culture and even their own language. Their conversations full of 'man,' 'right, man' and 'far out.' Just like listening to a trailer from the *Easy Rider* film.

It was a clash of cultures. I was a beer-drinking sports lover. An enthusiastic footballer and cricketer. My literary tastes included Ed MacBain and classics by Charles Dickens or John Steinbeck. Sports were anathema to most of the drug users I encountered. They were more Lord of the Rings than lords. I was Beefy (Ian Botham, an England cricketer and beer drinker), they were Captain Beefheart. I was the Beatles and the Stones. They were more Jefferson Airplane and Vanilla Fudge. I was conventional. They were unconventional. Therein lies the key to an animosity that exists to this day.

It's an animosity displayed by some in the drug subculture toward authority and police in particular. Many belonging to a drug subculture ferociously defend their right to do as they please. They perceive the police as 'pigs.' They see police officers charged with a duty to prosecute drug offenders as the enemy. They forget they are lawbreakers. Instead of working from within the system, they bleat about the 'war on drugs' from outside. These people also forget that many of these drug dealers sell to anyone. Their customers often include school kids.

These brief days on the Drug Squad in Hampshire did not fulfil me. Small-time dealers always whinging and whining. Looking back, I searched about one house or flat every week for drugs armed with a search warrant. Our finds included hash, weed, LSD and speed (amphetamines). Some of my colleagues were pathetic. Imagine getting excited about finding a roach in an ashtray? It was small town and small-time mentality – a far cry from murders in Lancashire. I wasn't a fit for the Drugs Squad but it would have to do for the time being. It was better than patrolling the streets in uniform.

I was acclimatising to the Hampshire dialect and the different ways of doing things, besides learning about the 'druggie' way of life. None of this was easy. The dialect thing worked both ways. I couldn't understand their Hampshire Hog twang. They were unable to decipher my Scouse.

My real goal was to return to CID, pronto. I had worked hard on my transfer from Lancashire to Hampshire to get out of uniform. I worked hard and smart. It didn't take me long to weigh up the existing CID at Basingstoke. That is where I ended up following my transfer from Lancashire. It is a modern London overspill town in the middle of rural Hampshire. The majority of the CID there acted bone idle. The laziest of them also had that knack of trying to make you feel inferior. I detest that attitude. The majority treated me with suspicion because they learned I had been an experienced detective in my former force. I don't think any of them put in a good word for me, in fact, I'm sure some spoke against me behind my back. An incident that happened while I was on the uniform night shift played into my hands.

At about 11 o'clock on a warm Saturday summer night in June 1974, a brawl took place in one of the Basingstoke pubs. One gang of ten young men had attacked another gang inside the pub. It gave me an opportunity to show my mettle. One young man went to the hospital to receive stitches to his face where he had been glassed by a rival. It all started following an argument about one of the gang members owing money for the purchase of weed.

The normal uniform police procedure would have been to seek witnesses to the attack. If a witness could say that an attacker or attackers were present, then an arrest would follow. They may also have made efforts to liaise with the hospital to seek further witness statements, both medical and from the victim. But the overwhelming desire on the part of most uniform officers in this situation would be to pass it on to the CID like a game of 'pass the parcel.'

The CID would then pick up the pieces the following morning. I arrived at the pub with two other uniformed officers. Our arrival coincided with the ambulance taking away the wounded youth. His face was a mess. The glass had left a wound some seven inches long and it was deep. I spoke to the landlord of the pub after the ambulance had left. He told me he knew all the attackers' names. Also, he knew the names of several witnesses to the incident.

Only one plan of action for me. First, to write a list of all the witness details so they could be contacted later to make a statement. But, more importantly, I needed to take a witness statement that night. It would include details of the attack and names. I found that witness in a young woman still at the scene. She gave me a full eye-witness account and the names of all the people involved. She knew them from her schooldays.

Once armed with the statement, I returned to the police station at about one in the morning. The uniform sergeant wanted me to leave matters there; to make a full report and leave it all to the CID for the morning. I persuaded him to let me have one officer and go and arrest the main culprits.

With a look of pained resignation, he agreed to let me do that. The rest of the night was busy. Knocking on doors, rousing the offenders from their slumbers and carting them off to the police station.

The sergeant intervened once more. 'Leave it now. Let the CID finish the work.'

I shot back at him, 'You have to be joking.'

Six young men had been locked up for a serious crime. I interviewed all six. They admitted everything.

Now six in the morning, I was sleepy after a busy night. Six is the normal time for the shift end – 'knocking off' time. I carried on preparing the court file.

The sergeant's last comment to me as he walked out of the door was, 'No overtime for this.'

Money did not interest me. I needed to get back on CID. The first of the detectives arrived shortly before nine o'clock. I waited for the first Detective Sergeant to arrive. In measured tones, I took him through the previous night. He nodded.

'What about the paperwork?'

That's when I placed the court file on his desk. It was complete. I felt like a magician pulling a rabbit out of a top hat. The file contained the lot – remand form, witness statements, crime report, confession statements, police statements, antecedent history of all the suspects, fingerprints and photographs.

He smiled and said, 'Paul is off to the Regional Crime Squad soon. You interested in taking his place?'

I had an ally, at last.

Before a transfer to the CID at Basingstoke took place, someone at HQ thought about the Drugs Squad. It proved to be a decision that altered the course of my life.

My own personal life in 1976 did not look too rosy as I was in the throes of a divorce from my teen sweetheart, Sue. She was the innocent party as – and not for the first time – my lower regions took over from my brain. I had started an affair with a Jilly Johnson look-alike. (Johnson was a well-known model in the 1970s.) I needed a respite from this tangled web.

### Life-Changing Phone Call

I sighed a welcome relief when I received a phone call from Dick Lee. He asked me to meet up so we could have a chat about his venture. Dick was an avuncular Yorkshireman and a DI in the Thames Valley force. I had worked on some joint drugs operations with the squad from Reading and had met Dick as a result. I must have left an impression. Peter Long also called me to ask me what the hell was going on. Peter had a right to know. He oversaw the Hampshire Drug Squad. Peter told me it was a potentially dangerous undercover operation. He added that Lee had backing from the top to handpick a squad.

These developments impressed me. And to be honest, I felt wanted. At the same time, I began to feel more than a little apprehension. The closest I had come to undercover work saw me spend time in a Portsmouth pub. The local Drugs Squad had a drug-dealing problem in one of the pubs on their manor. They could not keep watch as they would be recognised. It fell to me to watch the dealing in the pub. As an outsider, I wouldn't be known by the local dealers. I spent many evenings in that Pompey pub. It served as good training for Operation Julie in that I was paid for drinking beer on duty.

I had my meeting with Lee a few days after I got his call. He blew smoke up my arse as only people can when they are really pitching for something. But it didn't matter, he said enough when he explained that he had a special role in mind for me. That was the hook. He had me. I was also ready for a change of scenery in more ways than one.

Humdrum drugs work was getting me down as was Basingstoke, as was my tangled love life. Within two weeks or so of my meeting with Lee, my life changed. I started to drive a route that became so familiar to me over the next two years or so. I knew it as the road to Devizes in Wiltshire.

# SIX

# DEVIZES AND THE PHONEY WAR

Devizes is a county town in Wiltshire. It is close to Salisbury Plain, so it has a large military presence. It is also home to the Headquarters of the Wiltshire Constabulary. Dick Lee had chosen this place as the nerve centre of Operation Julie. Logistically it made sense as most of the action was to be in London and Wales. The town sits conveniently in the middle of those two locations. The Wiltshire Police HQ had the added benefit of adjoining a quiet road. The motley array of vehicles and personnel that would enter through its gates would remain incognito. Besides, it also possessed fine sports facilities and grounds. In the early formative days of the Operation Julie squad, we enjoyed many impromptu games of football. That is when my new colleagues discovered my passion for all things connected to Liverpool Football Club.

A game of rugby was also arranged by our Welsh contingent. Terry Stokes was a member of the Julie squad and had represented Wales at Under-19 level. Dai Rees was another who had played a good standard of rugby. Terry became our rugby captain, coach and chief bottle washer all rolled into one. He had played football with me and could see I could run.

He turned to me on the eve of the hastily arranged rugby game and lilted in that wonderful Welsh accent, 'You're on the wing, Steve boyo!'

I had never played the game in my life before, so I asked him what I had to do.

'Simple enough,' he said, 'catch the bloody ball and run like hell until you score a try or someone knocks the living daylights out of you!'

Well, I didn't manage to score a try but I definitely had the living daylights knocked out of me. It was a memorable day, though. We suffered an honourable defeat to an almost full-strength Wiltshire Police fifteen. I kind of regretted not playing the game when I was younger.

Many enjoyable social activities happened over these first few weeks. The best was when my brother, who lived in Canada, visited and a small group of us met up with him for a curry in Devizes. Following that we all jumped in a car and had an enjoyable road trip to Coventry to watch Coventry v. Liverpool. I liken this phase to a phoney war. Everyone knew the action would start sooner rather than later. But the time for bonding with new colleagues and training in new methods for some of us also had its place.

Graham Barnard, a Detective Sergeant, came from the same Thames Valley force as Dick Lee. Graham was a methodical and intelligent detective. He was quietly spoken, but when his mouth moved – you listened. He took responsibility for putting us through our paces in surveillance work. We used cars and other vehicles to follow targets – the tag given to suspects, either the suspects themselves or the vehicles that carried them.

There is a lot of technique and the learning of a new radio language involved. It was both fun and exhilarating to learn these new skills. It was even more exhilarating when we put these skills into real situations or 'follows' for the first time.

We also had to learn how to use an SLR camera. We had some good camera kit, including expensive Nikon camera bodies with telephoto lenses. The importance of being able to use such equipment is paramount. The operator may only have a second or two to compose and focus in on a subject of interest. That picture is potentially a vital piece of evidence in any future prosecution. It is worthless if the subject's face is out of focus.

One of Dick Lee's great strengths was he was a good networker. This is in an age preceding the present usage and meaning of that word. I think he invented it! He had an ability to locate and source all kinds of kit not normally available to police officers. His contacts in the Security Services unsurpassed and a source of constant amazement. We often ended up with equipment that was only available to Special Forces. Many upward curves happened in this time in relation to the learning process. We had nondescript vans used for surveillance left parked in strategic locations. Three or four personnel usually manned them, each taking a shift at acting as the eyes for the team.

We all had to learn how to cope with many claustrophobic hours spent in these vans while also having to learn the knack of peeing in a bucket. The 'knack' lay in one's aim. Yes, that included the ladies. Well, maybe not the aiming bit. There was no privacy within the confines of one of those hot stuffy vans. A pleasant distraction provided on one occasion was to watch one of the females strip off. It was a hot day. Even hotter within the confines of the van. She stripped down to her bra and panties. Luckily, she was one of the attractive policewomen.

One of the important features of these early days was a recognition. We were part of something big. Or to be more accurate, we were part of something that was going to be big. I was then, and now, a keen observer of people. I soon concluded that we had no passengers on board.

The Julie squad had no lame ducks. Every single man and woman was a highly competent detective. It lent credence to Lee's mantra that he had hand-picked all the personnel. It was also unique. It consisted of a hardcore squad of 25 detectives. We came from eleven police force areas throughout England and Wales. Of course, Regional Crime Squads existed in those days, but the clue is in the word 'regional'. The squad evolved into a de facto national drugs squad. It is such a pity the lessons were not learned.

## Plas Llysyn

Plas Llysyn is the name of a large imposing country mansion house just outside of Carno in Mid Wales. Accessible only via a long drive. The house itself is set in substantial grounds with a high wall. A stream coursed through the grounds. Nothing overlooked it. Whichever direction one looked there were fields, cattle and the sky above. Then a caravan arrived. A battered old caravan parked close to the entrance to the drive and next to the main road.

The phoney war days of Devizes were now over. Now for the first taste of real action. Lee had tasked a small group of detectives to conduct a surveillance operation. I was included in that group. Our task – to watch Plas Llysyn and its occupants. Lee believed the mansion to be the most likely bet as the location for the manufacturing of more than 90 per cent of the world's LSD. He thought of it as 'The LSD Factory'. It felt an honour and a privilege to be part of the small group chosen for this clandestine operation. Terry Stokes, Dai Rees and one or two others joined me. We were privy to the briefing by Lee when he spelt out the task ahead and filled us in on the details.

Excitement! I couldn't wait to drive to Carno and start the surveillance. Before setting up our observation post (OP) in the caravan, our group stayed the night in a pleasant B&B about 30 miles from Carno. We thought it necessary to stay that far away to not to attract too much attention from nosy locals. It was a comfortable place. The best part about it was the restaurant and the superb food it served. It was so good we decided to make this place our home from home. At least during the time we watched Plas Llysyn. Or that was the plan.

Dick Lee joined us for one night and one superb dinner. He was as impressed as the rest of us with the quality of the food and the locally sourced ingredients. But his mood switched and he forgot about his food as he studied the bill following the meal. After all, Dick was a Yorkshireman and folks from that county do have a reputation for meanness.

He barked, 'If you bloody lot think you are going to stop here for the duration and put these meals on your expenses, then you'd better think again!'

That was the end of that, and a search began the next day for cheaper options.

The towing caravan was a nondescript greying trailer measuring about 18ft x 6ft. It had been someone's pride and joy when new but was typical of those found on construction sites the world over. It contained a drop-down table and some old office chairs. We had a gas stove and kettle to brew our cuppas. Lee had managed to source some old draughtsman style plans and we laid those out on the table.

One of our crew had managed to scrounge a theodolite, level and some extending tripods. We seemed to be land surveyors. That was the idea. Our prepared cover story now built upon the idea of surveying the area in preparation for coalfield exploration. Our cover story further enhanced when the local postman delivered a letter to the caravan. Addressed to a fictitious surveying company care of the caravan, followed by the actual location as the rest of the address. Terry Stokes had addressed it and mailed it from Llanelli.

This was in the days when the Royal Mail was a functioning outfit and not the mess it is in now. The postman had no reason to know we had posted the letter to ourselves. The ruse no doubt served its purpose. Rural Wales is full of gossiping locals. The postman is a focus and one of the key figures in such a community. Unwittingly, he would have reinforced our cover as surveyors. Inquisitive locals may have interrogated him about us and the caravan. He would tell them about the letter.

The bulk of surveillance work is utterly boring. This watch was no different. For hours, sometimes days on end, there was nothing to see. Nothing happened. We saw no cars, no people. We had our binoculars and cameras with long lenses at the ready. They stayed redundant most of the time. No one passed by the caravan on the way to the drive to the house. All we saw for days on end were the cattle in the fields. Oh, and birds in the sky and the excitement of a flurry of traffic on the main A470 Carno to Machynlleth road. Occasionally, we heard the scream of an RAF fighter jet as it flew overhead. We later learned that the ever-innovative Dick Lee had arranged for the RAF to fly over the area to take reconnaissance photographs. The hope being that they may reveal some secrets of Plas Llysyn.

Sometimes relief from boredom came in the shape of a battery radio we had in the caravan. That was a blessing for me one Saturday afternoon on 4 May 1976. Why do I recall the exact date? My team, Liverpool FC, clinched the title that day. They scored three goals in the last twenty minutes of an away game at Wolves. It was the last game of the season. I listened to the whole of the commentary on the radio. It was good that the caravan was so isolated as I let out the mightiest of yells of delight as Liverpool scored. Three times!

Some occasional activity at Plas Llysyn did happen but it was few and far between, and it seemed to happen in spurts. One specific burst of activity took place over the space of a few days. We had taken many pictures of vehicles, occupants and the person who constantly went in and out of the front door of Plas Llysyn. We had the ability to shoot these photos day and night. We also had state-of-the-art infrared lenses and binoculars. All 'borrowed' from some secret government laboratory somewhere in rural England.

The negatives had to be sent back to Devizes for developing. This was pre-digital camera days. Only then could the subjects of the photos be identified. They were all connected to the LSD scene in one way or another. Some had a connection to the 'father of the hippie movement', Timothy Leary. We also saw Kemp and Bott on many occasions. Bott would leave Kemp at the mansion for up to 48 hours at a time. We had to exercise caution during this surveillance. A man, later identified as Paul Arnaboldi, was often seen scanning the drive for unwanted visitors. It was clear to us that acid manufacture was going on there at that time.

Another man, a mystery man, was also sighted. We never did confirm his identity. He was believed to be an armed and dangerous fugitive who had fled California. He had jumped a $50,000 bail in connection with manufacturing acid in the Golden State.

Suddenly the activity seemed to stop. A Mini Moke car driven by Paul Arnaboldi was frequently seen coming and going to the house. It was seen by us leaving on one last occasion and that signalled the end of the burst of activity at Plas Llysyn. On 8 May 1976, the Mini Moke left Southampton on the Bilbao ferry. Arnaboldi was now en route to Majorca. The imposing house appeared to be empty of all occupants.

Of course, Dick Lee remained in constant contact with us, eager to hear updates on what, if anything, was going on. We relayed to him that in our collective wisdom we believed the house to be empty. He gave us the go-ahead to nosy around the grounds to test our theory. So we nosed – several times, both at night and in daylight. We satisfied ourselves that our theory was correct. None of our sorties was greeted with any kind of response. The grounds and the house were silent. There were no lights on. No one was home. Time for a plan.

Lee had always been convinced that Plas Llysyn was the acid-manufacturing HQ. He was supported in that theory by Neville Dunnett, a Home Office scientist and drugs expert at

Aldermaston. Dunnett appeared to agree that this location had the hallmarks of being an acid factory. Lee's theory was reinforced following confirmation of the identities of the people we had photographed at Plas Llysyn, which included Paul Joseph Arnaboldi, the owner of the house. Kemp and Bott were also active. Lee now faced a dilemma at an early stage of the investigation. Should he order the raid to take place now and stop the production in the acid lab? Or should he hold off as the distribution network was as yet undiscovered? He chose to delay.

Arnaboldi was an acquaintance of Solomon and the early LSD guru Timothy Leary. So, there is a connection to the Brotherhood of Eternal Love. We later learned that Arnaboldi had bought a home in Deià, Majorca. Then he bought Plas Llysyn, on the pretence that he was there completing a biography of President Kennedy. He was at the top of the conspiracy to manufacture and market LSD. At the time of the Operation Julie swoops in 1977, a source said he was tipped off. He fled to Majorca where the Spanish police arrested him. But he was later released because no extradition treaty existed between the UK and Spain at that time. He then flew to America and disappeared. Some reports say he died in, Majorca.

Lee and our small group hatched a plan. We needed to break into the mansion to find evidence of the manufacture of LSD. We did some recces over the course of the next few nights to find a point of access. It would also help us determine what tools we needed to gain entry. Cellars or a large basement lay under underneath what would have been the ground floor. Creeping around in the dark of the grounds, we could see a wooden door that did not appear to have been in use for a long time. It was a sturdy thing with thick steel or iron hinges – our way in.

In these days of reconnoitring the house, or 'casing the joint,' the 24/7 surveillance of the house from our caravan continued. We could not relax in case there was an unexpected appearance or development. We now knew where to break in so we needed the tools to help us achieve our aims. We knew it was risky to buy our house-breaking implements in Carno. That may have aroused suspicions. Terry Stokes and I went shopping in Shrewsbury, a large market town in England some 50 miles distant, close to the Welsh borders.

It was a strange sensation. Law-abiding police officers on a jaunt to buy house-breaking tools! An uncertainty existed in my mind about the legality of our project. I didn't care. My attitude was one of – needs must, to hell with the consequences. In any event, I thought, the lawyers would sort out the technicalities if the worst happened.

Still, it felt weird. We entered a large Woolworths store to select our tools and placed them in the shopping basket. No one could read my mind, but I still felt a little sneaky. We went straight to the hardware section. There, we picked out long metal case openers, two hammers, screwdrivers, a drill and bit combo, and a quality flashlight. We also threw in several pairs of rubber Marigold gloves. We didn't want to leave fingerprints. Before we went back to our car, we also stopped in a camping store and bought four black balaclavas. We figured that if embarking on a potential illegal venture then we had better disguise ourselves. On our return to the cabin, we spread out our wares with immense satisfaction.

Someone asked, 'When are we going in?'

'What's wrong with tonight?' I said.

We approached the house the same night we bought our tools, in complete darkness at about three in the morning. There was no moon and I had difficulty seeing the others even though they were stood close. An eerie silence was punctuated by the odd snap of a twig underfoot. It was enough to make me jump. I instructed the others to wait a few moments, as I had an idea.

In hushed tones, I explained my idea and suggested that we all crouch down behind some shrubbery. They complied. I grabbed a handful of small stones. I divided them into approximately equal halves. I poured them from one hand into the open palm of the other, and, closing my fist over the remaining half, I threw with my right hand and aimed at the bedroom window. My aim true, and all present heard the clattering of small stones and gravel on the glass. The others started to rise from their crouched hiding places. I raised my finger to my mouth and hushed them. I thought if I heard a noise rousing me from my sleep, then I would probably ignore it and turn over in bed. Only if I heard the noise again would I take notice. I repeated the stone trick and again we heard the clatter.

After two or three minutes, I whispered, 'Let's go.'

A tentative shuffle down a slight grassy incline led to the cellar door. Terry Stokes and Dai Rees got busy with the screwdrivers on the door hinges. We did not want to use the case openers to wrench the door from its hinges. That would have signalled an unauthorised entry to anyone returning to the mansion. We were in! I volunteered to stay outside to keep watch, as I was the tallest of our group and most likely to split my head open on a low beam in the basement cellar.

The rest of our small team of covert operatives got busy with taking samples from the cellar. They included dust and residue from the stone floor, flaking plaster from the walls and pieces of wood taken from the beams and pillars. Every item was bagged as potential evidential exhibits. The team stayed in there for about 20 minutes or so before appearing at the cellar door. There was one last job involving a small-diameter pipe leading away from the cellar. Dai Rees scraped on the inside. He collected the glutinous and smelly contents. The pungent gunge was placed in yet another exhibit bag. One of the items turned out to be a dead rodent that had died of LSD poisoning. Those samples provided evidence of the existence of an acid factory in that cellar. Dick Lee was right all along.

# SEVEN

# ERIC AND UNDERCOVER PREPARATIONS

Carno was a wrap. There was nothing else to do there. Intelligence sources confirmed that Arnaboldi had fled, never to return. He was in Majorca. We were on to the next job.

Dick Lee called me and said he had a plan in mind for me. We arranged to meet at Devizes the day after I received the telephone call. I made that same drive from Basingstoke along the A303 to the end of the Andover bypass. Then a right turn and off toward Ludgershall and cross country to Devizes. The cross-country part of the drive is beautiful. Open roads and pleasant woodlands and fields on both sides of the road. It is British Army country and has many garrison towns dotted about the area. As I gunned my car through the sweeping bends, I had time to think. My thoughts turned to the imminent meeting with Dick Lee. It was a pleasant preoccupation. Nothing could spoil such a beautiful day. I rarely bet on anything. Yet, setting off in my car that day I'd had a brief conversation with a local in a village outside of Basingstoke. He was an elderly man. I saw him in the village newspaper shop.

He asked me, 'Do you bet, young man?' I was all ears because this was Kingsclere, an area noted for the Balding racehorse stables.

'On occasions.'

With that, he gave me the name of a horse running at nearby Newbury later that day.

'Put a fiver on it,' he commanded.

I did exactly as I was told. Later that day, I collected £40 in winnings. That put me in a happy mood, and I saw it as a good omen.

Lee called me into his office. He told me to grab a pew. Lee said, 'We'll wait a few minutes. I've asked Eric Wright in on this meeting as I have something important to say to both of you.' We waited for Eric to enter the office.

I had heard of Eric and knew he was one of the officers in the Operation Julie squad. I had never met him before. He had a couple of years' experience in Bristol city centre as a plainclothes officer. And a member of the Special Services Squad that specialised in combatting street car crime – a crime prevalent in that city. He had a reputation for being a solid no-nonsense thief-taker.

Eric walked into the office with that tell-tale rolling gait. Eric looked like an extra out of a movie about the Vikings. He sported long red hair with a matching red moustache and beard. He wore trademark faded denim jeans and a scruffy old jacket.

'Morning, guv,' said Eric to Lee.

Dick mumbled something back under his breath. I took a liking to Eric immediately. He seemed a friendly sort and appeared to have no airs and graces about him. We both waited for Lee to look up from his paperwork on the desk in front of him. He took his time. We remained patient.

'Right, you two.' The bark startled me. 'I have something special for the pair of you. It could be dangerous and if you want to say no then it's no problem.' Dick Lee knew how to grab my attention and arouse my curiosity.

He then outlined what he had in mind for us. It involved infiltrating a small rural community in Mid Wales. The plan centred on a village called Llanddewi Brefi. By way of explanation, Lee added that the area was full of not just the Welsh locals, sheep and mountains, but also a small army of dropout hippies.

Lee added, 'A man known as Smiles also lives in the village.'

This was the first time I heard this name.

'We think Smiles, real name Alston Frederick Hughes, is a key player in the LSD distribution chain and not too far removed from the top of the tree.'

Dick Lee clarified to us that Smiles remained our prime target and we had to do our best to get close to him and his social circles.

'I don't expect miracles. I'm sure Smiles won't let you too close and I'm bloody positive he won't confide in you,' Lee opined. 'I need eyes and ears on the ground. That's why I'm asking you two.'

We soon shared Dick Lee's opinion about Smiles's abilities. The intelligence on Smiles showed that he was experienced in the world of dealing drugs. He was too worldly-wise to trust two complete strangers. He was a product of the Birmingham and London drug scenes. And, he had mixed with some heavy hitters before he upped sticks and moved to rural Wales.

After outlining his plan, Lee said, 'Take your time. Let me know within a couple of days if you want to do it. If you do, then you'll need to concoct a cover story. I want you there in two weeks' time.'

Eric and I glanced at each other before we left Lee's office. I swear we both had the same stupid grin on our faces.

This development fell beyond my wildest dreams. Deep down I had no intention of turning down this opportunity. Alright, I did think about the danger aspect. I am unsure that danger is the right word. More fear of the unknown. I thought for a few seconds. I dismissed any apprehension from my mind. *Real undercover work at last!* I loved the movie *Serpico* and I wanted to be Frank Serpico. There was an element of potential danger. We knew of the story about a contract out for Martyn Pritchard, one of our other undercover guys. The bosses offered Martyn a semi-automatic pistol to carry for protection.

Would I have said yes to Dick Lee if I had known what lay ahead? Yes! I was young and loved the adrenaline kick of policing. I also believed at that time that I was doing the right thing. My part in helping society and the world to be a better place. How idealistic! How naïve! What I didn't know at the time is that there would be a personal price to pay.

Eric and I didn't need the two days' grace extended to us by Lee to decide. On leaving Lee's office we set up camp in an empty office on another floor of the HQ building. We talked to each other for two to three hours. There was no one else involved in our new venture. We had a task and carte blanche about how to perform it. This was the time I formed my opinion of the man who sat in the same room as me. It was an opinion never to waver during the entirety of our undercover days together. The same opinion is intact to this day.

Eric had a pleasant lilting Gloucestershire accent – a country boy style of lilt. It contrasted with my city-hewn accent. My dialect was still strewn with unmistakable Scouse from my years in Liverpool. I weighed him up. I had in mind Lee's caveat that there was potential danger involved. I stood about 6ft 3in and was on the slim side, save for a small beer belly. My legs were the type that went on and on.

Eric was the opposite of me. He was roughly 5ft 9in with a broad physique. He possessed wide shoulders above muscled arms and thighs like tree trunks. The Viking look of the flame hair and wild beard made him look scary! *This is a guy I can trust in a fight.* So I put my mind at rest about our safety in the event that things got rough. Just as important, he was a man I felt at ease with. He was a gregarious person who enjoyed a laugh. And he had a keen sense of humour and an engaging likeable persona.

As undercover school, or training, did not exist we had to make it up on the fly. If asked to write an undercover manual, this would be the first rule. If you worked undercover with a partner, you MUST be compatible. Compatibility does not mean you are clones of each other. Eric and I could be like chalk and cheese but we were compatible. We were a good mix, a team: Morecambe and Wise, Keegan and Toshack. Or, to use more recent examples: Suarez and Sturridge, even Ant and Dec! One British newspaper headline later dubbed us the Starsky and Hutch of the Valleys!

I knew little about LSD apart from the usual 1960s and 1970s tabloid headlines along the lines of people high on acid throwing themselves off tall buildings because they believed they could fly. All false, as I discovered much later. My hallucinogenic drugs training took the form of me reading the Carlos Castaneda book[9] about the Yaqui and peyote. I enjoyed it and later found it useful to employ as a talking point when in the right company.

Eric and I, during our bonding chat, decided to let Lee know we were in. Why waste any time? He wanted us in place in two weeks so there was a lot to do. Lee had a big grin on his face following our announcement that he could count us in. Crafty old sod! He knew we weren't going to refuse.

The initial chat between the two of us resulted in the sudden realisation that this was serious shit. We had a lot to do to prepare for the infiltration of Llanddewi Brefi. I needed to learn to pronounce it and spell it, for one. As I said, no rule book or manual existed to guide us. We used our common sense and a pooled cunning intuition. Part of that intuitive nature compelled us to spend most of the next two weeks in each other's company. We had much to do and much to learn about each other.

We had to shed off the cloaks of Steve Bentley and Eric Wright. We needed new identities. The identities were one of the easiest parts to fix or at least the physical aspects were. Before you create a new paper identity, you need a new name. I have no idea to this day what process we used to choose our new names – Steve Jackson and Eric Walker. You cannot carry your real ID with you when you go dark. A police warrant card is out of the question.

We spoke to Lee about our new IDs. In no time at all we each had a driving licence in our new names. This man had connections! We pushed him on one further issue and he saw the force of our argument and arranged it: false Criminal Record Office (CRO) files connected to our new identities. Nothing too serious, just a drugs possession bust or two. Additionally, in my case, a minor conviction for assault. It was important not to show jail time. If either one of us had claimed to have done time in prison that would have been a recipe for disaster. We would not have been convincing to anyone who had served time in real life, particularly when it came down to a discussion about a specific nick (prison).

Prisons are close, and of course closed, communities. Everyone who has served time knows someone, who knows someone, who knows someone else.

There was another valid and pressing reason for the fake IDs. This was the 1970s. Corruption was rife in certain departments and squads of London's Metropolitan Police. If we infiltrated this Welsh village, we did not want to run the risk of discovery. We aimed to get close to Smiles and the drugs distribution network. A bent, corrupt police officer could have been on the payroll of anyone connected to this drugs cartel. Furthermore, we could not risk the chance of a local Welsh bobby checking us out as a favour to one of the locals. This was just as corrupt in its own way, but not on the scale of the copper who is on the payroll of a criminal gang.

The local Welsh police officer is another key figure in rural communities, just like the postman at Carno. The less these local cops knew, the better. Sometimes, the cop's wife would also know everything about her husband's work. That could involve a potential for danger. Too many loose tongues abounded in these communities. In 1975, before Operation Julie, Lee and Detective Sergeant Richie Parry worked together. Parry was in charge of the Dyfed-Powys drugs squad. They believed that Smiles had a stash of over a thousand LSD tabs hidden in his home in Llanddewi Brefi, which fell under the Dyfed-Powys jurisdiction. A search party combined of both local officers alongside a selection of Lee's set off to raid Smiles's home at Y Glyn. The uniformed Llanddewi Brefi officer went with them. Things went awry before they arrived. The local officer's wife had walked the short distance from the village police house to Y Glyn. That was maybe fortunate for Smiles, possibly unfortunate for the police.

She knocked on the front door of Y Glyn. A bemused Smiles greeted her.

'Is my husband here? I have a message for him.'

She returned to the police station on receiving a polite, negative answer. Smiles could not believe his luck. She had unwittingly forewarned him about the impending raid. A short time later the raiding party arrived to find relaxed Smiles and no sign of any drugs. They left disappointed and empty-handed.

They later discovered the wife had received a call from a police colleague of her husband. He was trying to get a message to the local cop. At first, he called Aberystwyth station, the venue the combined force search team had gathered for a briefing. The team had left for Llanddewi Brefi so he called the colleague's wife to pass on his message.

That message began, 'Your husband is on his way to Y Glyn so can you please pass this message on to him there.'

Keystone Cops! Or *Police Academy*? Take your pick. It was indicative of the slackness and lack of professionalism in those parts.

One of the keys to going undercover is to keep as much truth about yourself as you dare to. I kept my real date of birth.

Let me illustrate why. Imagine this scene – 'Oh! I thought your birthday was last week,' says the guy who has just picked up my fake driver's licence. I, having dropped it by accident – '... it says it isn't for another couple of months on here.'

Eliminate the unnecessary risk! I also retained my Liverpool background. I figured it was a large enough city that it would not present any problems. Little did I know then that Steve Jackson and Eric Walker would spend some time in the great city of Liverpool. They were nervous moments for me, but more of that later.

During those two weeks, Steve Jackson and Eric Walker bonded even more. We sure got to know each other. Discussions turned to the reasons we would give to be in such a rural area of Wales – Llanddewi Brefi. Eric took the lead in those discussions and I was happy for him to do so as he came up with a great idea. An idea later tested over and over. Its implementation was key during our time together as Jackson and Walker. It never failed.

Trevor is the name of Eric's younger brother in real life. From what I gathered, he leaned towards the harum-scarum type of character. Nothing too serious, and never charged with any criminal offences but he was often in minor scrapes of some kind or another. The fabricated story revolved around Trevor having been busted for a minor drugs possession charge. Having been bailed to appear at court, he failed to appear and a warrant issued for his arrest. Trevor, having absconded, was now missing, but thought to be living in a hippie commune somewhere in Mid Wales. Eric, being the concerned elder brother, and at the behest of his dear mother, had promised to try to locate him. Like it? We did, and it worked a treat.

Things still needed ironing out in the rest of our cover story. One of them was to satisfy curiosity about how we made money to exist. That took a little bit of thought. Both of us had a love of cars and enough knowledge between us to pass as car dealers. We came up with the story that we bought and sold cars using the auctions at Southampton.

This was a double-whammy benefit. One, it satisfied nosy folks who wondered how we earned money. Two, it gave us a reason to leave the scene for a while, for a few days or even a week. Remember I said that Eric was a country boy? He had a petrol-driven chainsaw we always carried with us. That became another source of income and a cover story, and we once even cleared a whole bunch of trees for some hippie dude near Lampeter.

There were two more important matters to which to attend. We needed wheels. Neither of us was keen to use our own cars. We persuaded Lee to give us a budget of £500 to buy an old van. Eric took charge of the purchase. He came up with a pale blue Ford Transit diesel engine van. It was the perfect choice. Old and a little rusty in places, and inconspicuous, at least until Eric's partner Jan had the bright idea of painting garish psychedelic flowers on the side.

Shades of San Francisco, flower power, hippie love and peace, man! I wasn't too sure and thought maybe it was a little too much. But all who saw it seemed to accept it. The only person ever to mention it was Smiles. And even then, he was piss-taking and not an unbeliever in us and our stories. The Van, as it was affectionately known to us, served other useful purposes too. It carried the chainsaw around wherever we went. We also carried our sleeping bags and two mattresses in the back. It became our home for the gloriously hot summer of 1976.

The other important matter that needed attending to was my appearance. I looked too straight. Too regular, with hair not long enough and little facial hair. My clothes were casual in style, but too smart-looking. I had thought this within days of saying yes to Dick Lee. A casual chat with the lovely partner of Eric's Jan, reinforced my opinion. My recollection about my appearance when I first met Jan is at odds with her recollection. I recently discovered she has a journal:

> *Eric was partnered with Steve, also long-haired and bearded; a tall, quiet man, outwardly gentle and soft-spoken but with a brooding undercurrent that gave me the impression that if he hadn't seen it or done it he knew all about it. They were to work together undercover, form a close relationship and come to depend on each other totally. I felt they were both in good hands.*

During the two-week bonding period with Eric, I had spent some time in his home near Bristol. There I met not only

Jan but her beautiful daughters, Nikki, Lisa and Sarah, along with Jack – a Jack Russell Terrier that I adored. Jan made the best cheese and onion sandwiches I have ever tasted. Thick slices of real bread. Huge chunks of extra-mature Cheddar cheese and eye-watering onions. All washed down with a mug of tea.

I recall Jan pointed out the deficiencies in my appearance to me during one of these sandwich sessions. She is a considerate person and did it with tact. But she was right. I immediately ceased shaving and cutting my hair.

At one point, my hair fell way beyond the middle of my back. I visited a flea market. I bought some faded denim jeans, two jean jackets and some cheesecloth shirts. I also bought some cheap metal rings and started to wear them on my fingers. There was one more thing to do before setting off for Wales in the van for the first time. I dirtied my jeans on purpose. They needed to look well-worn. And I added the odd strategic tear to complete the desired effect. These clothes were my uniform for the next nine months.

# EIGHT

# LLANDDEWI BREFI

The van had been in the workshop at Devizes HQ for the past few days. The mechanics there did a great job of servicing, greasing and giving it a thorough check over. They gave it a clean bill of health and one fine sunny morning Eric and I set off for Wales heading for Llanddewi Brefi.

We had false driver's licences and a fabricated criminal record. It seemed only right and proper that the van joined us in our grand deception. Lee again pulled some dark and mysterious strings. The van now bore a completely different ghost licence plate than the one it ought to display. The records were also changed at the Driver and Vehicle Licensing Authority (DVLA) in Swansea. We were now safe with the van. The official DVLA record showed Eric Walker as the owner with a fake address in Southampton. That is what any corrupt police officer would see. That would be the report back to his criminal paymaster. That is what we wanted.

The summer of 1976 proved to be one of the hottest and most glorious summers on record in Britain. The morning we set off typified that summer. The temperature in the morning was about 23°C and rose hour by hour to a high of about 33°C later in the day. The skies were crystal-blue clear. These days went on for months. The only rain came with the odd thunderstorm, which was a welcome relief to the heat of the day. We cooled the van on the journey by the simple expedience of winding down both the front windows. The wind blew through one side straight out the other. Both driver and passenger then had to flick long hair away from the eyes time and again. Surely a price worth paying for the cooling effects of the breeze.

We both smoked in 1976. Back then I used to smoke tailor-made cigarettes – just a regular brand in a twenty pack. Eric was definitely a roll-your-own man. His adroitness at hand-rolling a cigarette was compelling to behold. He could do it while driving. He would produce the tobacco pouch and grab a small amount of it. Then he would peel off one Rizla cigarette paper. Place the tobacco inside the paper and roll the perfect cigarette. All while holding the steering wheel with the other hand. Eric's hand-rolling ability would prove to be useful in the days and months ahead. At the time of setting off for Llanddewi Brefi neither of us were, nor had been, drug users. Not even the odd toke of weed! That changed in due course and became a necessary part of our temporary new lives.

Typical of policing at that time, the authorities expected us to infiltrate a drugs cartel with no training in undercover techniques. No training manual existed. And no psychological assessment to determine your fitness for such demanding work. In due course, my naïvety in the practicalities of smoking a joint could have been a fatal flaw in our cover story. It could have led to our unmasking. I adapted and was able to control the situation. I even turned it to our advantage, but only through force of personality and natural ability – not training.

The road trips to Llanddewi Brefi never became tiresome. But before that first trip, we needed to figure out where to keep the van. We decided it would be folly to keep it at Devizes. The sight of the hippie flowers on the side of the van would prompt curiosity, even among the most stupid of people. To drive it in and out of Devizes on a regular basis was a no-no. We left the van parked a walk away from Eric's home in Bristol. Far enough away from his house to prevent anyone linking Eric and the van. There were people who may have known Eric as a police officer. I would drive my car to Bristol and leave it close to Eric's house. Our visits to Devizes would become infrequent, partly by choice and partly through exercising our discretion. We had a carte blanche and 100 per cent freedom to operate as we saw fit. In effect, we operated as a lone wolf, but plural rather than singular. We would be seeing action behind the enemy lines.

The drive from Bristol to Llanddewi Brefi first took us over the Severn Bridge along the M4 Motorway, the most boring part of the trip. To avoid that boredom, we often took the A470 and then the A40 from Abergavenny to Llandovery. From there we would drive to Lampeter before taking the last few miles to Llanddewi Brefi. Lampeter became the 'last gulp of air' pit stop. Then we plunged into the depths of our undercover activities.

We found a decent greasy spoon café in Lampeter that did a fair all-day breakfast. It had the classic plastic red gingham tablecloths. Not to mention the generic tomato ketchup bottles filled with the cheap ketchup. At least they didn't fill Heinz bottles with the cheap stuff as many places did. It also had a jukebox in the corner playing the hits of that time. The Eagles 'Take It to the Limit' was on there. And also a song we came to adopt as our signature tune – 'The Boys Are Back in Town' by Thin Lizzy. The next nine months changed me in so many ways, including adding to my taste in music.

The first time we did the trip, we talked non-stop about who we now were, practising our lines for the big performance to come. I had an idea partway through the journey.

'Let's pick up a hitchhiker, Eric.'

'What the fuck for?'

'So we can mutilate him and kill him,' I said deadpan.

'Oh! Fuck off! I'm serious – what the fuck for?'

'Dick shit, why do you think?'

'I don't fucking know Scouse git. That's why I'm asking!'

'So we can practise our story on him.'

'Fuck me! You're a genius!'

We saw our victim hundreds of yards away. We could see him walking along the roadside with a backpack slung over his shoulders. Even from the rear, he looked exhausted, weary and thirsty on this hot summer's day.

'He'll do,' I said.

Our victim, the lone weary traveller, was about 25 years old. He said he was from Manchester but studying at a college in Lampeter. He was intelligent and chatty. More to the point, he asked us loads of questions. The answers flowed from both of us. It was a performance worthy of an Oscar. To us, it was more valuable than that trophy even though they are gold. It gave us the confidence to be our new selves. I had heard some years before that a lie becomes more convincing with repetition. The author of the lie can, and often does, come to believe the lie. The charade with the weary traveller did just that. There was a hidden compartment in the brains of both Eric Walker and Steve Jackson. Those secret places bore indelible stamps and each stamp read the same – 'You are not who you thought you were. You are who you are now and who you say you are.'

Eric and I, and the van arrived in Llanddewi Brefi on the evening of 3 June 1976. We immediately headed for the New Inn, a small pub in the village. The pub was almost empty. Three customers took up a corner table. All sounded like locals and were of no interest to us. They spoke almost non-stop in Welsh, pausing only to gawp at the two strangers in their midst.

We did have a chat with the landlord and his wife, mainly to the wife. She appeared to run the pub. She seemed anxious to find out who these two strangers were that had drifted into her pub. I thought of her as a friendly sort and it didn't feel like we were subject of an interrogation. This was the second opportunity we had that day to put our cover story into effect. She seemed to accept the story of Eric's brother. We became regular customers of the pub and she never failed to extend a warm welcome, often making a polite inquiry on the progress in the search for Eric's brother.

We never became accustomed to the locals chatting away in Welsh in the pub. On the odd occasion, they would break into English. There are certain English words that have no equivalent in Welsh. It sounded weird to hear a local placing an order over the bar chuntering away in Welsh. That is until he got as far as ordering smoky bacon crisps. As a rural area, the village suffered from power blackouts. If that happened in the pub, it was common for the banter in Welsh to stop. There would be a deafening silence, broken by, 'Fucking street lamps!' English words spoken in the strongest of Welsh accents.

# NINE

# SMILES

We decided to pay a return visit to the New Inn the day after our arrival. As I went into the small, cramped bar lounge area, I could not fail to notice one person already in the pub. He sat at the bar, perched on a stool, in the company of another man. He turned to face the entrance as soon as Eric and I walked in. The shock of black hair and the white teeth were immediately recognizable. I had seen the photographs of Alston Frederick Hughes in the files at Devizes. Smiles! And yes, he smiled. This guy could smile for England and win a gold medal for smiling!

Smiles was about 5ft 8in and a proportionate build. He had black wavy hair, long sideburns and a moustache that all joined up. There were tattoos on both arms with the word 'Smiles' on his left forearm. He had a tanned face and white teeth. You needed sunglasses looking at the dazzle. An earring adorned his right ear. He spoke with a slight Cockney accent, although he hailed from Manchester. He had the general appearance of a market trader and could pass himself off as a gypsy. He wore a bold tartan check shirt and corduroy pants. He introduced us to Buzz, who sat next to him at the bar.

Buzz did little talking. Smiles was friendly and chatted away. He told us he was soon going to London to buy a VW camper van and tour Europe for a month. We practised our cover story for the third time. It was by now not so much practice because the script just rolled without effort from our mouths. Before we parted company that evening, Smiles offered to take us to the Red Lion (Y Llew Coch in Welsh) pub. It was in nearby Tregaron. He mentioned it to help us find Eric's lost brother. He added that the Red Lion was where it was all happening. And the "faces" in there, as well as the landlord, may know something. Our tale seemed to be working, much to our relief.

Once we had parted company with Smiles and Buzz, we headed back to the van. After driving about a quarter of a mile, Eric and I turned to each other and beamed big smiles of satisfaction and relief. It was less than 48 hours following our leaving Devizes in the van for the first time. We had met our target, Smiles, and his companion Buzz. Before this encounter, a million things went through my mind. In the main, they took the form of searching questions.

'Would we find Smiles?'
'Would we get close enough to talk to him?'
'Would he accept our cover story?'
'Would he accept us?'
'Would he like us?'
'What will he be like?'
'Can I go through with the charade?'

These questions and thoughts were spinning around my head. It was constant. No answers, just thoughts and questions. Like many things in life, it was a case of fear of the unknown.

After meeting Smiles, I felt the greatest relief. I knew I could do this and not only do it, but I could enjoy the lie. I experienced a deep inner feeling of release. I revelled in the new me. I now know this feeling was a cerebral reaction to a lifetime forged by my upbringing by a particularly strict father. I was now disinhibited and carefree. I had thrown off the chains of deep-rooted insecurity layered into my psyche caused in no small part by my father. I was going to have fun!

There was ample time for thinking and reflection in my early days in Llanddewi Brefi. The interaction with others was not constant. There were times we drifted off in the van toward seclusion and isolation. Those moments were of great value. Llanddewi Brefi is not a large place by any standards. It is a village on the road between Lampeter and Tregaron. It had a couple of pubs, a church, a village store, a village hall and a police house. It was a source of irony that the police house, occupied by the local bobby and his family, was close to Y Glyn. Smiles lived at Y Glyn. Fields and mountains surrounded the village. We found seclusion higher up from Llanddewi Brefi on the mountain slopes. This was a time and a place to relax, eat, bathe and discuss the job in hand.

We found an ideal place to park the van overnight. It was a good two miles or so out of the village and on the ascent to a rough mountain road. This mountain road would have been a drovers' trail in years gone by. It led to a man-made dam and lake known as Llyn Brianne. The van occupied a small parcel of uneven stony ground set back from the road. It was next to a copse and a fast-running stream. The stream was full of clear mountain water and served as our private bath. The morning ritual was bathing in the stream; the pure clean waters were just fine to drink, too. The rear doors of the van fully opened up, to grab the early morning cool breezes. A curious observer would have seen our mattresses and sleeping bags.

A portable gas stove was also on view, as well as a kettle for our morning cuppa. Once the kettle boiled and was poured into the mugs containing the tea, it was time to fry up. Bacon, local fresh eggs and sometimes a prime cut local steak were the regular fare for two hungry guys. There were fish in the stream. Eric was the country boy and I was hoping he was able to tickle trout out of the water as poachers do. He tried but failed. The only downsides to this otherwise idyllic location were the mosquitoes and horse flies. A horse fly bit me on the thigh while I was washing in the stream. My thigh swelled up to the size of a tennis ball.

It was rare to see anyone up in our regular overnight spot. We did see an occasional local farmer passing by in his beat-up Land Rover. A wave in friendly acknowledgement was all the communication we ever had with him. The locals were familiar with the sightings of incomers and hippie-types.

They thought no more of the two bearded hippies in a flower power van than they would be seeing cattle or sheep in a field. The animals would have been of more interest to the farmer.

The hours spent in our spot recharged our batteries. These were hot summer days, and on exploring the rugged drovers' trail we stumbled upon a rock pool. It was the perfect spot for skinny dipping on a hot day. The mountain waters were both invigorating and cold. Those feelings of nudity and lack of inhibition also fed a sense of freedom. I loved the golden silence up in the mountains. A silence that was only interrupted by the odd low flying fighter jet. The RAF pilot honing his low-flying mountain terrain skills. This habitat of rocks, boulders, rough mountain grass and high peaks was perfect for the red kite. It had almost become extinct in the British Isles. Daily, we saw a pair high on the wing above us as we lay back in the grass after a swim in the rock pool.

A telephone kiosk stood at the side of the road as we drove back toward the village from our mountain retreat. From there, and others dotted about the area in secluded locations, we made our daily report back to Devizes. Collie was the mainstay of the admin staff in the Operation Julie Squad office. She was an experienced civilian member of the Wiltshire Police. One of us would make the call, reversing the charges, and it was Collie who answered without fail. She would answer, and then call out, 'Steve and Eric!'

Collie's shout was for the benefit of the Admin Inspector, Brian, in charge of the office, or Julie Taylor (the Julie in

Operation Julie) if Brian was absent. He or she would know if Lee wanted us or anyone else had an important message for us. If there was nothing of any urgency for us, Collie would say, 'Right, I'm ready.' And ready she was, to take down in shorthand the contents of our daily report. We would talk and she would annotate. There was never an interruption from her. Never a social nicety, never a need to repeat anything; she was super-efficient. Collie then transcribed her notes into a typed document that we knew as the Llanddewi Brefi Log. At the conclusion of Operation Julie, I asked her for a copy of the log. I am using it to help me provide you with an accurate account of events from years ago.

A typical humdrum and early entry from it reads:

*8 June 1976*

*Back in LB the day before. We gave a lift to two hitchhikers and dropped them at a hippie commune with wigwams at Llethyr Coch. Sid Rawles has been staying there but most people have gone to a festival in North Devon. We learned that this year's big festival is to be held on a site in Sherwood Forest.*

*Last night we went to the Red Lion at Tregaron to see the licensee as Smiles suggested speaking to him about the long-lost brother. There we met an interesting character (not yet identified) who claims to be a friend of Smiles. He was going to the Continent with Smiles but has backed out. Buzz is definitely going to the Continent with Smiles. The*

> two of them had worked together previously on a building
> project. The landlord at the Red Lion is called Ianto. Smiles
> is definitely still in London. We met another interesting
> character in the Red Lion, a Scot called Angus.

I did say earlier that most detective work is routine. The same applied to our new roles as undercover officers in our new environment. Much of the work was regular intelligence gathering. Socialising in furtherance of spreading our cover story. And of course, drinking copious amounts of beer. I bet you like the sound of that part of the job! All the while we were masquerading as Steve Jackson and Eric Walker, car dealers, nice guys looking for Eric's errant brother.

# TEN

# BLUE

On 10 June 1976, we met Blue and Mac. They were in the New Inn and we got into conversation with them. We did not know then that Blue was to play a big part in our undercover future, an exciting part. And on one occasion, a downright scary part! Mac, in his own less prominent way, also had a part to play. We recounted our cover story to them over a couple of beers in the New Inn. A story so natural now, I completely believed in its authenticity.

Mac and Blue must have been okay with the cover story too. All four of us left to continue our drinking and socialising at Blue's home, a house he rented in the village. Blue was about 27 years old and claimed to be from the East Midlands. Yet, he had a transatlantic accent. It turned out he had lived and travelled a lot in Canada and the United States. He was a six-footer, stocky with a barrel chest, dark longish hair that had a touch of early grey at the sides. A ginger moustache perched on top of his mouth. He was an engaging character, a man I warmed to immediately.

Back at his home, Blue regaled us with tales of New York, Los Angeles and Miami. It was clear he knew these locations well. He dropped names like Ken Kesey, the author of *One Flew Over the Cuckoo's Nest*, and Timothy Leary as if he knew them as friends. Perhaps he did? Blue was the first person to talk to us in depth about acid (LSD). He went into detail about the acid travelling labs in California. In particular, he talked about the selling of LSD to the Hell's Angels on the west coast of the States. This was the story of the Brotherhood of Eternal Love. Blue had the gift of the gab, openly admitted, and it attributed it to his Irish roots.

Mac was the complete opposite of Blue. He was about the same age as Blue. Where Blue was stocky, Mac was haggardly skinny. His thin pale white skin stretched across a bony frame. He had the sharp facial features of a weasel, light brown hair worn collar length, and a pendant earring in his left ear. Mac lived outside of the village, on the road toward the youth hostel. He was fond of his weed and showed us a two-ounce weight wrapped in polythene. He hid it in his trousers. I did wonder about the bulge in his pants until he showed us the bag of weed! All four of us had a pleasant, chilled evening.

Our routine became one of using our mountain retreat to bathe and breakfast. Refreshed, we would drive up the mountain road to explore the beautiful landscape. Once, we made it as far as Llyn Brianne. There, we marvelled at the man-made waterspout spewing thousands of gallons fifty yards or so up into the air. We never failed to use our rock pool for some nude swimming to escape the heat of the midday sun. Then, it was time to work. The pubs were open.

Blue became friendlier by the day, acting as an unofficial guide to the area and an introducer. He took us to a house at Llangeitho to meet an American who wanted to buy a transit van like ours. On reaching the house, neighbours told us the American had gone to London for the week. Yet, it wasn't all bad news, as this attempt by Blue to help with the sale of a van could only mean one thing. He believed our cover story. He thought we could accommodate the American by sourcing and supplying a van. If necessary, we would have done just that.

On returning to the village from the abortive trip to Llangeitho, Eric, Blue and I headed straight for the New Inn. Smiles had returned from London. He hadn't yet gone home since returning. Several shopping bags lay on the pub floor beside him. He was eager to show us the expensive-looking new clothes he had bought in London. He was with a big guy from Liverpool. A well-dressed fellow who, like Smiles, enjoyed throwing his money about. They were both buying drinks for everyone in the pub. Smiles repeated he was going to buy a VW camper to tour Europe and would soon go to Belgium to buy it.

The big guy tried too hard to compete. It seemed like he was trying to outdo Smiles. There was only one winner in a popularity contest. Blue got as pissed off as us by the show-off from Liverpool. Someone mentioned the Mick Jagger film, *Performance*. It was showing at a village hall in Pontrhydfendigaid. Blue asked us if it was of any interest. He didn't need to ask us twice. We agreed to go with him.

• • •

The small village of Pontrhydfendigaid was like a scene from Woodstock. There were so many heads, as in acidheads, potheads, etc. The three of us made our way to the village hall main door. The film was due to start at ten o'clock. It was still daylight as we arrived on Midsummer's Day, 21 June 1976. A massive gorilla stood guard on the door. He looked out of place with his shaven head among all the hippie hirsuteness. The individual tattoos on his forearm were bigger than my fist! We got in with ease, even though we were complete strangers. Once inside, the smell of patchouli oil and marijuana filled the air. There must have been between 100–150 heads in the hall waiting for the movie to start.

I lost count of the number of lit joints. There were men, women, boys and girls, and toddlers. Almost all wore typical hippie-style fashion – loose tops adorned with Indian beads, and many of the men sported waistcoats with vivid floral patterns. Old Levi jeans filled the room. About half the men wore a hat of some description with fedoras being among the most popular. There were many male ponytails. The females often wore their hair long and in varying stages of unkemptness.

We took a seat at the back of the hall and were immediately accosted by a girl who looked about 20 years old. She was pretty with long blonde hair tumbling down to her waist. She wore a cute see-through white cheesecloth top. I could see the most perfect small but rounded breasts with large, erect pink nipples. I tried to make eye contact but failed.

'Mushrooms', I heard her say.

Not the kind you fry up for breakfast; she had psilocybin, a hallucinogenic. To decline was not an issue.

All three of us said 'No, thanks,' and she moved on. I hoped to see her sometime again soon, but I never did.

We watched about three-quarters of the movie. I became restless and bored so I told the others I was off to the kitchen area of the hall to see if there was any beer. Eric and Blue followed. There was a skinny kid in there, no older than 16, rolling a huge joint. I asked him if there was beer and he nodded toward the refrigerator. There were about 12 cans of beer in there. I grabbed three. I passed on two of them to my buddies, leaving a bit of change on the worktop that should have covered the cost of the beers. We stood about in the kitchen until we finished our beer and chatted to the kid. Or rather, he chatted to us. He seemed to have a lot to say.

He was friendly but completely stoned. The only way to describe his utterances is utter gibberish. He thought he had solved the problems of the universe. The only trouble was he had extreme difficulty in communicating the solution. From time to time he would pass us the giant cone of a joint. Blue was with us. We all had a few tokes, then took off. Next stop was the Black Lion in the village. I was still thirsty and, even more so now as I began to discover that dope made my throat dry. The landlord of the pub was keen not to miss an opportunity to increase the takings over the bar. Even though it was late, he continued to serve what seemed like the entire hippie population of Wales.

In Tregaron, we also got friendly with a local guy. He lived and worked in Tregaron but that is all I am prepared to reveal about his details. I do not wish to identify him and the reason for that will become clear. I will call him Happy. He was a trusting soul and was open in his nature and in his speech. He was far from being stupid. On reflection, I believe he was trying to spice up his own life living in such a rural community. None of what he told us was ever acted upon as we never knew what, if anything, was true.

Happy told us Smiles had any amount of LSD at any given time. We knew they were on friendly terms because we often saw them together and there was a bond between them both. Before the end of June was out, Happy volunteered some information. He told us Smiles and Buzz had gone to Amsterdam to deliver acid to a painter who lived in that Dutch city. We asked no questions to prompt that revelation. He volunteered it. Happy had backed out of the trip after Smiles and Buzz invited him to go along for the ride. Or maybe it was to be a trip within a trip?

He added further detail saying that the other two would make £5,000 each. His cut was to be £2,500. From Amsterdam, the plan was then to go on to Munich. He admitted to scoring acid on a regular basis from Smiles and selling it in Aberystwyth. That was the largest nearby university town. He would either sell for or make 50p a tab profit. He wasn't clear on that point. Happy offered to get us a sample from Mary, Smiles's wife, that day. He called this latest batch Spangles and described the tab as a raised silver oblong.

Happy went on to claim that he scored his dope from Mary's ex-husband. He was John Preece, from Birmingham. Happy added he could score any amount he so wished. I should correct something now that I said earlier. I said none of this information was acted upon. On reflection, I do not know whether any of it was fruitful. The raids and busts that ensued as a result of the Operation Julie investigation were huge in numbers. I never knew the full details or saw a list of those arrested. I saw no list of premises and/or vehicles raided and searched. There were over 800 police officers throughout the UK involved in the dawn raids in 1977. They were synchronised raids. I do know that John Preece received a custodial sentence for his part in the distribution network.

Blue had moved to another rented house by the end of June. It was a remote stone house in Silian at the end of a narrow farm track. We became frequent visitors there. Blue was proving to be invaluable. He introduced us to places and people in the head community for miles around. These were people we would only have met if we had stayed undercover there for the next two years or so. He seemed well connected and well respected by his peers. As a bonus, he was friendly with Smiles, our prime target.

# ELEVEN

# STONED

The days of living in the van extended into weeks and then months. Winter would be approaching, and we had to think of an alternative to living in the van. The seclusion of our mountain retreat was fine in summer. The bathing stream and the skinny-dipping rock pool would soon become cherished memories. The cold and damp of a Welsh winter were on the horizon. The daily routine carried on for a while yet.

The van was incomplete without the presence of Eric's chainsaw stowed in the back. Through Blue's introductions, we had two sidelines. Both gigs involved receiving cash or a gift in kind as reward for our services. Eric could use a chainsaw with skill, confidence and ease. We, or rather Eric, pruned and cleared overgrown trees on two or three occasions. I watched, kind of supervised really.

We also moved furniture or personal effects for various people in the hippie community on many occasions. Sometimes Blue was with us and helped. Other times it was just the two of us moving stuff from one secluded house to another. Many of these 'customers' were hippies. The reward was usually a fiver (£5 note). In 1976, it was a reasonable payment for a couple of hours' work. Occasionally, the reward would be a small gift of weed.

The most memorable day moving stuff in the van was the day we did Blue a favour. No money or other reward was either offered or asked for. It was one of the funniest days of my life. Blue had asked us to pick up a piano from a house several miles away. He had bought it and now had to find a way of getting it back to Silian. We went with him one morning to collect the piano. It was one of those upright pianos and it was damn heavy.

The four of us managed to load it into the back of the van to a backdrop of much grunting, groaning, sweat and some colourful language. It overhung outside the back of the van so we lashed the van doors open to their fullest extent. The piano was also secured on the inside of the van to keep it upright on its journey. An upright piano should always remain upright.

There was no room in the back for the piano stool and a couple of occasional chairs. The hippie seller had thrown them into the bargain. We lashed the extra furniture on top of the van, but with great difficulty as the roof had neither a roof rack nor anywhere else to tie down the ends of the ropes. We improvised by knotting the rope ends to the door handles of the van to the rear and the door hinges of the front doors. This was better than nothing but it meant that we were unable to fully close the front doors of the van. The rope prevented the doors from closing shut.

## ELEVEN

We set off Silian bound with our cargo in the back and on the roof. Eric was driving, Blue sat in the middle. He had the gear stick between his legs. I cramped up next to the passenger door. Both front windows on the van were wound down all the way. It was yet another hot day of the summer of 1976. Our travails in loading the van and securing it were exhausting. A call for refreshment now in order.

Blue knew a pub halfway back to his home at Silian. We walked out of there about three hours later. Blue, Smiles, Mac and even Happy were all seasoned consumers of drugs, not to mention seasoned drinkers of beer and liquor. Jack Daniels, Bacardi, vodka, whisky or whiskey – Scotch, Irish or bourbon, it did not matter. They did not discriminate. I was always fond of beer but I was now drinking all the above in increasing quantities. I had also got used to smoking both weed and hash. When offered, I would oblige and inhale two or three times and pass the joint on in time-honoured custom. All three of us had drunk plenty and smoked enough weed in the pub that day to make me feel stoned. The landlords of that area never objected to pot smoking in their premises. If they did, then they would have had few customers left.

All three of us were stoned by the time we reached the long narrow track that leads to Blue's home. The van lurched up and down, side to side over the potholes and loose rocks of the track. It was like riding a drunken camel. I was still cramped up next to the passenger door. I had urinated at the pub before we left but felt an urgent need to go again.

Once you start peeing after a drinking session, you never stop, right?

I hinted to Eric a couple of times that I needed to stop and go pee. In his stoned mind, he must have found that hilarious as he just cackled. When stoned, and in the company of stoners, laughter is infectious. Often no one knows what they are laughing at, it just feels good. But I did need to go!

'For fuck's sake Eric. I need to piss!'

'Okay, okay, I'll stop.'

He braked to a sudden stop. So sudden, the passenger door fell off the van with the rope ends still attached to it. The roof cargo – the piano stool and chairs – had slid off the roof towards the back and were now hanging off the side of the van! I had been squeezed up against the passenger door when it, and me, parted company with the van.

I heard convulsions of laughter. Eric and Blue, still seated in the van, were looking down on me sprawled on top of the disconnected door. That and the swaying loose furniture were the sources of amusement. It was enough to send three stoned hippies into more fits of laughter. The howls and hoots ceased after about three minutes. Was it three minutes? Who knows? We were wasted! I was lying on my back on top of the errant, disconnected door when I saw a cow about three yards away. It was up against the farm field fence and staring at me. Cow eyes filled with curiosity or amusement?

'What the fuck you staring at, big eyes?' I yelled at the cow.

I added, 'Got nothing else better to do? Go fuck a bull!'

Eric interjected with his country boy wisdom – 'It is a bull. You prick!'

That did it. The lull in gales of laughter now over. The noise of mirth and merriment coming from the three of us must have carried some miles distant. We were beyond caring!

Sometime later, we edged toward Blue's home. I know not whether that was three, five or 30 minutes. Time becomes distorted by smoking good weed. Eric drove down the track advancing little by little. It was all done in slow motion. We had left the disconnected door at the side of the track along with the chairs. On arriving, we gathered ourselves together to heave the piano into its chosen spot. It was to sit on the stone floor of the living room.

Blue's lady, I'll call her Lily but that isn't her real name, said 'Hi' and asked what I had been up to. She noticed the dirt and dust covering my clothes. All three of us burst out laughing once more! She shrugged and walked away.

Blue later recounted the tale of the door and the cow for his Lily's benefit. She then busied herself with cooking a meal for the three of us. While Lily was cooking, we went back and retrieved the door and chairs, this time placing all the debris into the back of the van.

There were maybe two hours to kill before Lily had the meal ready to serve. We sat outside and smoked another joint. Then washed it down with some poitín (Irish moonshine) Blue had brewed a month earlier. It didn't take long for the fits of laughter to start up again.

A five-barred gate stood between Blue's home and the track. I initiated an Olympic sport of jumping the gate. It was my idea so I was first to go. I took a walk to the track-side of the gate and measured out my run in my inebriated mind. I ran and jumped. A kind of scissor-kick type jump. My leading leg cleared the gate, as did my bum and upper body. My brain did not communicate with my trailing leg. It caught the top of the gate and for the second time that day I was the source of howling laughter.

There was more dust and dirt on my Levi's. We ate our meal, drank some more, smoked some more and listened to music. Blue got his guitar out and strummed some good stuff. We were as high as the proverbial kites. Blue got around to riffing some chords and singing a chant-like verse. Eric had commandeered some tom-toms he found behind a sofa. That was my cue to start chanting Native American style:

*Wee hee nah wee hee nah hee nah*
*Wee hee nah hee nah*
*Wee hee nah*
*Wee hee nah hee nah*
*Wee hee nah hee nah*
*Ay ho!*

It didn't make sense then and sure doesn't make sense now. No one cared! We stayed the night at Blue's and left the next day.

# TWELVE

# MOVIE STARS, ROCK STARS

The stories abounded of rock stars and other celebs who had either visited or lived in the area. It was while we were in the Red Lion, Tregaron, one day that Happy asked us to go to a party with him. When he mentioned it was at the home of Michael Wilding Jr. and there were plenty of chicks there, I was in. It turned out to be an uneventful day.

A London connection of Smiles, a man named Doug, was of interest to us. Devizes and Dick Lee were anxious to identify him as he was part of Smiles's distribution network. An associate of Smiles told Eric and me that Doug was likely to be at the Wilding party. He wasn't. But it was a further reason to go to the party near Devil's Bridge.

I did meet Michael Wilding Jr. at the party, and it intrigued me to meet him as the son of Elizabeth Taylor. She was one of the most talked-about movie stars back then. Her tempestuous relationship with her then-husband, Richard Burton, was renowned. Their antics were cannon fodder to gossip columnists and paparazzi the world over. She was often dubbed as the most beautiful woman in the world. I had read many articles about Liz Taylor that mentioned her violet-coloured eyes.

I spoke to Michael Wilding Jr. for some time as I chugged on a cold beer. He was a pleasant, softly spoken young man about six years younger than me. He seemed unfazed by who he was, or rather, who his mother was, and I did not bring her up in the conversation. What I did notice about him above all else were his eyes. They were the most stunning eyes I had ever seen in a man or woman. They were violet, but shone with a luminosity that was a little unnerving. I had the vicarious sensation I was gazing into Liz Taylor's eyes.

• • •

Jeff was a guy Eric and I had seen hanging a shop sign in the street in Llanddewi Brefi. He became another conduit to us meeting the music stars of the day. We struck up a conversation with him in the New Inn. It centred on his art and design work. The shop sign we had seen him hanging was his work. It was good. We learned that he had a connection to a beautiful lady called Pam. She was later going to let a house to us which was to become our base. Not only for the winter months, but also for the rest of our undercover days in Llanddewi Brefi.

Pam was the ex of John Mayall of the Bluesbreakers fame. A band that at one time included both Eric Clapton and Jack Bruce. Jeff's artwork must have been known in the London-based music industry of the 1970s. He approached us and asked us to take him to Kent to deliver a commissioned painting, a large mural, to the home of Ric Lee, the drummer of Ten Years After fame. He or his wife had commissioned the mural.

We agreed to take Jeff and the painting to Kent, for a fee. We never saw the painting. Jeff wrapped it in a shroud. Before we got to Kent the plan was to stay overnight in Pam's London home. It was in Orme Square opposite Kensington Gardens. We did stay there and Pam and John Mayall's adopted son let us in. He was living there. It was a pleasant evening. The son and Jeff were convivial company and I learned a lot about music owing to their shared love of blues music.

The son left partway through the evening. Eric thought he said he was going to the corner, like popping out to the corner shop. But he didn't return.

It was later realised he actually said, 'I'm off to see Alexis Korner.'

Korner was a family friend and often referred to as one of the founding fathers of British blues music. In the 1960s, Korner formed Blues Incorporated, a loose-knit group of musicians with a shared love of electric blues and R&B music. At various times the group included Charlie Watts, Jack Bruce, Ginger Baker, Long John Baldry. It also attracted a wider crowd of younger fans, some of whom occasionally performed with the group. They included Mick Jagger, Keith Richards, Brian Jones, Rod Stewart, John Mayall and Jimmy Page.

We were in illustrious company. One of Pam's London neighbours was also well known. He was Jeremy Thorpe

MP, the leader of the Liberal Party. He later became notorious during the 1970s. The 'Thorpe Affair', as it was dubbed by the press, was a British political and sex scandal that ended his career as the leader of the Liberal Party and MP for North Devon.

Our van looked conspicuous parked among the Rolls-Royces, Bentleys and Lamborghinis. Those luxury cars are common currency in this part of Bayswater. The following morning, we took breakfast in Queensway then strolled along to the Portobello antique market. Pam had a stall there and a successful business dealing in antiques.

We finally departed for the village of Smarden in Kent to deliver Jeff's work of art. The famous member of the married duo wasn't present. His wife was, and she was most welcoming despite appearing occupied by her work. I got the impression she also had some connection to the music industry. She was keen to keep a constant eye on her fax machine as she was expecting something important from California. If I'm not mistaken, she was American. She showed us to the guest quarters and our separate bedrooms for the night's stay. I didn't know we were going to stay overnight but thought, *Hell, yes, I can cope with this*.

They had a beautiful house afforded by the years of success achieved by the Ten Years After band. It looked old and had that half-timbered look so popular in the affluent villages of Kent. The guest rooms were en suite but there was also a communal WC on a landing. It was fantastic.

There were so many interesting prints on the walls. There were also a wide variety of reading materials to use while sitting on the loo. My bedroom had a comfortable bed, which was appreciated after many weeks spent sleeping in the back of the van.

I made my way down in the morning expecting us to hit the road and find an eatery somewhere on the road. I was at the foot of the stairs when I heard a call – 'Waddya like for breakfast? We got eggs, pancakes, bacon, sausage, toast.'

I couldn't see the American lady, but I heard her call out.

Eric went along with my choice – 'All five, please.'

After breakfast, we made the uneventful journey back to Llanddewi Brefi. We deposited Jeff there, a happy man. On the return trip, we had stopped at a Little Chef for a bite to eat and a cuppa. He could not contain himself any longer. Delving deep inside a pocket he pulled out a folded piece of paper. He unfolded it as if it was precious and caressed it like a new lover. Holding it between forefinger and thumb, he drew it between the two digits so it opened up. He kissed it then showed it to us. A cheque made out to him for £800, the price of his work of art. I thought *I must buy some paint brushes!*

. . .

Back in Llanddewi Brefi, we settled back into the regular routine. The trip to London and Kent had been a welcome distraction. It also acted as a further boost to enhance our credibility in the area. News travelled fast in these parts. We were still in the middle of one of the longest heatwaves on record in Britain. That gave us an opportunity to spend a day at a festival in Rhayader in the neighbouring county of Powys. The festival was held in the Elan Valley in the middle of nowhere. It was full of tents and tepees when we arrived. The tents and tepees were arranged around a central area. A makeshift stage kitted out with sound equipment occupied the middle. There were many mobile stalls selling everything from veggie and vegan treats to hot dogs to beads and clothing.

Some open fires were dotted about with cooking utensils perched on top of the blazing wood. Heads of all shapes and sizes wandered about. Some were clearly zonked! Ages ran from toddlers, even babes in arms, to men and women who appeared to be in their sixties. I guess there were about 200 people present. This was one of the free festivals, meaning there was no admission fee.

The parking area was full of the typical hippie forms of transport: VW campers and old converted buses, ambulances and Post Office vans. The men and women were walking about in varying degrees of undress. Some were naked, including one guy cooking over a fire. I silently wished him well, hoping the cooking oil didn't spit in the direction of his manhood.

There was no live band while we were there. We could only hear taped music blaring out, including Hendrix, Janis

Joplin, the Doors, Bob Dylan, Cream and other popular music. People, mainly young women, were swaying in rhythm to the music. Some of those women wore nothing or next to nothing. I sat down on the grass to watch and take in the music – ha!

There was silence in the van on the return to Llanddewi Brefi. For my part, I was still thinking of all those naked women.

Eric asked, 'Why have you got a stupid smile on your face?' I smiled some more and shrugged.

## THIRTEEN

# INTERNAL POLITICS

These days of high summer were just tickety-boo, enjoying life and work. How many times can a person truthfully say that in their lives? We had started to get close to Smiles and even closer to Blue. We filed our reports daily to the Devizes office by telephone and Lee was happy with what we were doing. Of course, he didn't need to know everything! I admired Dick Lee as he had many good qualities as a man, a leader and a detective. I suspected he was a little prudish. Maybe stemming from his early upbringing? He would not have appreciated knowing everything we were up to in Wales.

All we encountered accepted our story. The long-lost brother, the car dealing and just being two likeable guys about town. The car dealing cover story took care of our possession of a considerable amount of cash. We kept it folded away. It was our money, not supplied by Dick Lee or anyone else. Some of it was a result of our part-time removal and tree-lopping activities.

The bulk of the money was from the expenses we submitted on a monthly basis. We never asked for receipts, for the obvious reasons. It was a matter of trust that what we said we spent we did spend. We had the extracurricular activities of removals and tree-lopping. But we also tried to create an air of mystery. I believe it worked. We wanted people to wonder about us. Are they, or are they not, drug dealers? Some people did approach us on many occasions. They asked us to supply drugs, so I guess it worked.

The car dealer cover was perfect. It accounted for us flashing cash. Have you ever met a second-hand car dealer that doesn't have a bulging fold? It also allowed us to leave for breaks. The world of Llanddewi Brefi believed we had gone away for two or three days to attend to the car business. In reality, we were doing other things. A home visit was one and a check-in at the Devizes office was the other. The latter was important for two reasons. By far the most important was the filling in of our expenses claim form. We filed them in Devizes but then forwarded them to our respective police forces. Detective Inspector Peter Long, who was in charge of the Hampshire Drugs Squad, received my claims. He would sign it off then the payment would be made with my monthly salary cheque.

In the early days, Peter Long telephoned me one day while I was in the office at Devizes. He was anxious at signing off what were considerable claims.

'Look, guv,' I told him, 'I'm living 24 hours a day away from home living a life as a different person. I'm spending money as part of my cover.'

Peter queried, 'Why all the bottles of whisky?' No doubt scrutinising my claim form.

'I'm an alchie,' was my facetious reply.

Then, thinking I had best explain on that point, I added, 'These guys are heavy-duty drinkers as well as druggies.'

I did not think for one moment my joke about being an alcoholic would return to haunt me one day. The chat cleared the air. I received my expenses without fail and without queries every single month.

The average wage in Britain in 1976 was £72 per week. My expense claims alone were in the region of £40–50 per week. It was my flash money and it helped bolster our cover story. DI Long and others may have believed I was exaggerating these claims. I can't blame them for thinking that. It was impractical, given my circumstances, to ask for receipts. If they did harbour such a belief, I believe they also thought it was fine to go along with it and they treated it as an unofficial undercover allowance. There was no such thing as an official undercover allowance. Police chiefs failed to understand the nature of the work. They had no idea it could be stressful. They had no idea of the potential dangers. I don't think they cared.

The same internal political wrangling applied to overtime payments. Eric and I were living the lie. We were away from normality for 24 hours a day. Our salaries paid for eight of these hours. Our pay was for a 40-hour, five-day week. And anything over that daily eight hours was overtime. We were nominally asleep for eight hours in a day. So, we calculated we would claim for eight hours of overtime every day we spent in Llanddewi Brefi.

Pressure mounted on the squad to reduce their claims for overtime. That came from the chiefs of all the individual forces. Wiltshire Police went as far as ordering Fred Pritchard not to work on a rostered rest day to save on overtime payments. It was crazy. The needs of this operation dictated what hours an individual detective had to work. For example, to complete a surveillance task, he or she couldn't just drop tools and walk away. It was even more difficult for me and Eric. 'Excuse me, Smiles, we won't be in the pub tomorrow because it's a rest day!' We did not reduce our overtime claims at any time despite the pressure to do so.

Monthly briefings were a feature of the squad at Devizes. Eric and I got to as many of them as possible. It was good to keep updated with progress, or otherwise, from other members of the team. It helped me form a picture in my mind about the organisation of this LSD cartel we were investigating.

From time to time an outsider would attend these meetings. On one occasion, Nigel Dunnett from the Home Office Aldermaston laboratory came. He was there to explain some things about the actual manufacturing process of LSD. Derek Godfrey from Scotland Yard, the only Metropolitan Police officer Lee trusted, also showed up once. On a few occasions, the US Government Drug Enforcement Agency's (DEA) man in London would attend. I will always remember him for the long, Pink Panther-like detective's raincoat he wore. I did not see him ever remove it – even in the office. It was always belted and collar up. I always think Peter Sellers in *The Pink Panther* when I recall the man from the DEA.

The main focus of attention at these briefings was the surveillance on Kemp and Bott. Over time it switched more to Henry Todd and Seymour Road. This was after the discovery that Todd bought the house in Seymour Road using a fictitious name. The distribution network of Todd, Cuthbertson, Fielding and Spenceley was of great interest to Eric and me. Smiles was one rung down the distribution ladder from Spenceley. Russ Spenceley also lived in Mid Wales and supplied Smiles. These briefings were also an opportunity for us to keep updated with developments on the telephone intercepts.

We sensed the politics at these meetings. We were all aware the chiefs realised that they had unleashed the beast. We were in uncharted waters, and the organisation and policies were not in place to cater for what we were doing. A combination of funding concerns and petty jealousies fuelled internal politics. The petty jealousies were on the part of some chiefs of the individual forces.

The increased presence of Greenslade was a sign of the pressures on Dick Lee to produce results. Greenslade was in charge on paper only. In the early days, I never saw him. I had heard about him but he was like a spectre in the mists. He started to make more appearances at Devizes, but only after the bosses questioned the progress of the operation. I believed he had received a rocket from on high and was told in no uncertain terms to find out what Lee was up to.

**FOURTEEN**

# ARE YOU GUYS COPS?

There was a steady routine to our daily and weekly lives in Wales. It was only broken by those visits to Devizes for the briefings. We had duped the great head population of Llanddewi Brefi, and people like Smiles, Blue and Happy. They now all believed we had gone off to buy and sell another car to fund our lifestyle. All was good. Or was it? Eric and I spotted Smiles at the side of the road in Lampeter. It was another hot summer's day. We were driving back to Wales from Bristol. Eric stopped the van. We asked Smiles if he wanted a lift to the village. He did and jumped in the front of the van. I shuffled over to the middle. Eric was the driver. Smiles sat alongside me next to the door.

The van was still in first gear when I heard 'Okay boys. What's the scam?'

The words tumbled from the chasm between the smiling teeth. There was no warning. No 'Hello, boys. How are you?' It was a deliberate ploy by Smiles.

I froze. For a few milliseconds, I froze. My brain and stomach turned to ice. I was more worried about Eric's reaction. It's not that I couldn't trust Eric, but this had the hallmark of a first serious challenge to our cover story.

*Was this leading up to a direct challenge?*
*How would I react?*
*How would Eric react?*

You must think quickly when undercover. You must be alert and on your mental toes.

'C'mon you can tell me. You're cops, right?' came more words spoken through those trademark smiling teeth.

I responded before Eric. I hooted with laughter and said, 'You what?'

Smiles declined to follow up on my query. He was his usual amiable self all the way back to the village where we dropped him off outside his home, Y Glyn. He talked about Amsterdam and the Rolling Stones concert at Knebworth. He talked about Joan Armatrading and Steely Dan. He claimed to have been Armatrading's cannabis supplier in his Birmingham days. It was like he had never challenged us and our cover! As the years have rolled by, I look back at that incident. I believe Smiles was fond of pushing buttons in search of a reaction. I don't believe for one minute he thought we were cops. That was borne out by later events. It was just a part of his survival instincts. Whether I am right or wrong about that, it startled us.

The first challenge to your cover is the hardest. You learn that it comes with the territory. It's how you handle it that is the key. There is no advice I can give in how to handle it. It is a natural-born ability. You either can or you can't. The truth is that it depends upon so many different factors as to how you react to it. Laugh it off? Be aggressive? Ignore it? These are all options. You can only determine the best option by the players involved and the context. The one option not open is to admit it.

• • •

The social side of the head lifestyle was in full swing in Llanddewi Brefi and the surrounding area. A gig was arranged for the village hall to raise funds for some guys busted for drugs. Blue was heavily involved in those arrangements. We took him to a nearby village to collect some sound kit for the band that was due to play.

He was also instrumental in arranging a hippie football match that took place in the village. I was content to volunteer and happy to show off my football skills. Blue was still showing us around and acting as the introducer. He introduced us to some other local guys. The rumour was that they were active in the Free Wales Army, a group that had links to the Irish Republican Army and Basque terrorists. It had claimed responsibility for some firebombings of homes in Wales. We had no interest in them whatsoever. We had been made aware of the presence of some of their members in our first briefing before we ever set foot in the area, but it was more to instruct us to exercise caution as they had access to firearms.

The heatwave had gone and the winter was fast approaching. It was time to consider an alternative shelter to the van and our mountain retreat. Lee was understanding and authorised us to find a place to rent as long as it wasn't The Ritz. We asked around about places available for rent. Naturally, Blue was one of those people we asked. The quest for four walls and a roof later led us to Pam and Cartref.

### Gangsters and A Death Threat
### 1 September 1976

We had been in Wales in our undercover role for a day or so short of six months. At three o'clock that day we pulled up outside Blue's house at Silian. He looked in an unusually heightened state of agitation. We had no need to query the cause of his agitation. He narrated a complete story about a friend called Bill to us.

He pointed to a telegram laying on the dining room table, explaining he had received it that day. It was a request from Bill to go and meet him at the airport in Liverpool. Blue explained that Bill lived in Vancouver and had first flown to the Isle of Man. Then he planned to fly on to Liverpool. The rest of the tale tumbled from Blue's lips along these lines:

Bill was a wealthy guy and Blue knew him as both a friend and co-worker while he was in Canada. He was so wealthy he had recently sold a boat for $200,000. Bill was now looking for a suitable replacement boat. He was seeking a fast motorboat. Blue asked us if we could all go to Liverpool to pick him up. Eric and I agreed.

# FOURTEEN

Fast motorboats interested us. They were often used by drug runners to collect contraband ditched in the sea. Light planes would jettison the drugs into the water. It was a common method used as part of large-scale drug smuggling. Of course, there may have been an alternative explanation that was far more innocent, if not to say mundane. We needed to find out more. Eric went off with Blue to use a friend's telephone because Blue had no phone in the house. Blue called the Isle of Man number Bill had put in the telegram but not before showing Eric the contents of the telegram on the journey to make the call.

When Blue and Eric returned, I learned that we were to set off for Liverpool in the van there and then. We left Mid Wales at about five o'clock. The arrangement was that we would all meet up with Bill at The Feathers Hotel. It was a hotel I knew in Mount Pleasant, Liverpool.

It had been a warm and beautiful day, but nightfall had arrived as we drove into Liverpool. It had been one of the first of the Indian Summer days signalling the end of the glorious summer of 1976. We had driven through the Mersey Tunnel in our Ford transit van on our way to the hotel in Liverpool. Inside my head, I was happy but apprehensive to be back in Liverpool. It's where I grew up and had some happy memories from younger days. I was apprehensive in case I bumped into someone who recognised me as Steve Bentley.

I had taken over at the wheel before we got to the Birkenhead side of the Mersey Tunnel. The rationale being that I knew Liverpool like the proverbial back of my hand. We were heading for the hotel in Mount Pleasant. It was a stone's throw from the famed Adelphi Hotel, but much farther downmarket. I drove the van along Lime Street. A police car appeared alongside and flagged me to pull over and stop. I obeyed. We had no dope on board, or at least I didn't. I couldn't speak for Eric or Blue. But I had been drinking on the way up to Liverpool earlier that day. In fact, it had been quite a session in a country pub somewhere in Shropshire. The locals thought we were a rock band owing to our faded denim and long hair. We didn't disappoint them, telling a tale that we were London-based session musicians. That's what happens when you go undercover, you become adept at lying!

The uniformed Liverpool City Police officer didn't like the look of us. He asked a few questions of me as I was the driver. Every answer I gave him was a lie. After a cursory search of the van, he allowed us to carry on. But he first checked us and the van out with CRO (Criminal Records Office) over his radio. CRO was a national police database set up in 1974 for all matters related to crime and criminals. Our credentials stood up to the test. Our fake past criminal activity was relayed to the Liverpool officer. Yet, there was nothing on the database to warrant him arresting any of us. Blue also came up clean. It made me wonder later whether he was who he said he was.

On arrival at the hotel, the receptionist told us to go to Room F where Bill had checked in. Blue knocked on the door and after a minute or two a man, about 33 years of age, opened the door. His frame filled most of the door. He spoke with a distinct Canadian or American accent. It was a bit difficult to tell which. Bill and Blue hailed each other and hugged like long lost friends. Bill ushered us into his room. The hotel and the room were a little down at heel. It was a seedy dive, in truth.

Bill appeared ill-suited to such a place, based on the cut of his clothes. He wore an expensive shirt, casual trousers and slip-on shoes – the type with the tassel on top, and they looked handcrafted in somewhere like Milan. His suitcase was also incongruous with his temporary surroundings. It was a top-of-the-range Samsonite leather suitcase with matching attaché case. Bill and Blue chatted about places in Canada and people they knew in common. They were catching up.

Our host was generous, offering us drinks from a personal stash of Bacardi, scotch and vodka. They talked. Eric and I listened and watched. We nodded if asked for an opinion on something. Bill was well groomed with fat chubby hands. The broad build bulged into a beer belly at the waistline. There were no visible marks or tattoos. He possessed a round face with a pock-marked complexion. The marks suggested he had acne problems in his younger days. He had black curly hair worn short and well cut. He would not have stood out in a crowd. Bill was a heavy drinker. We had several good shots on the rocks and he was setting a frantic pace. Bill pulled out a nasal spray and indigestion tablets and lay them on the bedside table. The drinking appeared to affect his constitution.

We listened with a casual ear. Casual but full of purpose. The mind concentrated. It was intent on storing away all the contents in our respective retentive memories. Bill was talking about the sale of his expensive boat and about people he knew who were importing large consignments of drugs from the Caribbean to the US. Bill needed a change of scenery.

He said, 'Let's go out.'

We walked out of the hotel and turned into Lime Street.

'Pint of Guinness for me,' I said as we walked into the American Bar in Lime Street.

Blue went to the bar and ordered my pint. In fact, he had bought most of the drinks on the way to Liverpool as his way of saying thanks for the ride. But on this occasion, Bill handed him a fistful of £20 notes before Blue left our table. We got settled in the corner of the bar. It was a dirty, greasy table that had seen gallons of beer spills in its lifetime. The beer mats stuck to the veneered top. They made a 'glooping' sound as you tried to reposition one.

'These are the two guys I was telling you about,' Blue said to Bill as all four of us sat at a corner table in the bar.

Bill sort of grunted. We carried on sitting at the dirty table, Blue now doing most of the talking. I weighed Bill up, taking a good look at his face and his eyes. He had cold grey eyes like a dead fish. There was no glint, no soul, no expression in them. Just dead. Bill would turn his gaze on to either

Eric or myself. The only word that could describe his stare was sinister. I was thinking *This guy is a serious player.*

The chat, mainly by Blue, carried on for about an hour. During that time, I learned that Bill, although a Canadian, spent most of his time in Miami, Florida. Bill also confirmed that he had been searching for a fast motorboat. The search had taken him not only to the Isle of Man but also to Panama and the south of France. I was drinking my beer throughout and also drinking in Bill. Time flew, and I was starting to think ahead about where we could carry on drinking. It was getting toward that time when it was too late to wander into a pub unless you were in the know and could find a lock-in.

I had been away from Liverpool for too long to have that intimate knowledge. And besides, I would not want to risk my cover walking into a boozer that I knew well and where the clientele knew me (the real me) well. The pub idea faded. We all decided we needed to eat and I knew an Indian restaurant in nearby Bold Street.

The drinking and conversation carried on throughout our curry meal. Bill had now regained the lead role in the talking stakes. He was telling Blue how desperate he was to find a fast 80-foot boat. Bill spoke to us directly for the first time:

'Listen I've got an operation going over in BC involving snow, not any old shit. I've got my markets but, nothing over here. Coke is pure, straight from Bolivia. Retails at $24,000 a pound. If you guys are into that sort of bread, then I may be your man. What do you say to that?'

Blue interjected, 'Listen Bill these two guys are my friends, now we're out for the night so let's not talk about this.'

'Excuse me, excuse me, Blue, Blue, Blue – let the guys think about it and sleep on it.'

There was no more conversation about cocaine in the restaurant. But we did have a conversation with the friendly waiter. He gave us a quick guide to clubs to go to, including one where there were hookers and even told us the prices. He mentioned the She Club. I knew it and we decided to go there. The waiter arranged for a taxi to take us there. The only problem I foresaw was getting past security, as it was late. We weren't members nor did a member go with us to sign in at the door. Also, we had to factor in that Eric, Blue and I looked like members of a rock band. Some may have said we looked like hippies with our long hair, beards and denim.

But there are always ways and means. I did the talking, as I had the Scouse accent. In my pre-undercover days, a sight of my warrant card would have guaranteed entry. But that was Steve Bentley, not Steve Jackson. My Scouse pleas did not impress the security gorillas. But then I glimpsed a fist reaching across toward the chief gorilla. The fist belonged to Bill. It contained at least three £20 notes, maybe a week's wages for these guys. No one spoke another word. In place of words, the chief gorilla bowed his head and gestured with his arm in a sweeping motion in the direction of the entrance. We were in!

Two things I would never forget happened once we were inside. I started dancing but I had kicked off my shoes and was on the wooden dance floor. I had always wanted to dance barefooted and now I was granted my wish! It helped that I was inebriated. I had no sooner got on the dance floor and started to sway solo to the rhythms when I saw a good-looking, vivacious young woman. She was a brunette, slim, and wearing a pencil skirt that showed off her hips and legs. She joined me on the dance floor and smiled.

She laughed a lot. I liked that. I liked her. Her constant glances at my feet made me feel a little uncomfortable. I maybe have the ugliest feet in the world.

But she simply said, 'I have always wanted to dance with a guy who kicks off his shoes and dances barefooted.'

Yes – she really did say that! I liked her even more!

We danced for a while and when the slow stuff came on, we got cheek to cheek. She smelled good, too. I could feel her hips push into my groin and my other brain reacted, pushing hard against my denim jeans. I think she liked that. She started to thrust at me and grind her hips to the beat of the music. The beat was slow and sensuous. By way of small talk, I found out she was a nurse at a local hospital and was clubbing with her friend, also a nurse, on their night off. She had all night free and threw in for good measure that she wasn't in any rush in the morning either! I thought … *You know what I was thinking!*

Some time later the two of us made our way over to the table where Eric, Blue and Bill were sat drinking and talking. It was a dark corner table with a faux candle-shaped wall lamp giving off a glow. My new friend called out to her co-worker to join us. We now had a six-some! The girls went to the bathroom to powder their noses. We four guys started to chat among ourselves. This is when the second unforgettable thing happened.

While I was away on the dance floor, Eric, Blue and Bill had clearly got around to talking business. And by business, I mean drug smuggling. Eric later told me this was the gist of the conversation between him and Bill:

Bill asked Eric, 'You guys are into a bit of business with shit, right? You'll have to think about what I said.'

Eric answered, 'Sounds a bit heavy to me.'

'You must have a man somewhere?' queried Bill.

Eric responded, 'It's no good me saying yes or no until I've seen him though, is it?'

Bill continued, 'Sure, Ginger – we're talking about a lot of bread now, and in the future. Talking of bread, do you know anyone who will handle jewellery?'

'Warm?' Eric asked.

Bill shot back, 'Hot.'

'Not really my area,' Eric replied in a non-committal mode.

Bill then carried on telling Eric about a con trick to make $100 a day through his version of ringing the changes. Then he reverted to the topic of cocaine. Telling Eric how he paid couriers $500 a trip, evading customs by using fast boats. Eric listened and made a mental note of it all. There was also talk about legitimate businesses based in places like Nassau,

Barbados, Antigua, Argentina, Panama, Miami, Georgetown and Vancouver Island.

I had missed all this because I was getting hot on the dance floor.

But no sooner had the girls left us than Eric said, 'Ask him. I'm sure he will be okay with it.' He nodded at me.

I'm thinking, *What the fuck is he on about!*

Blue spoke up.

'Bill wants to know if you two can organise bringing a few keys (kilos) of snow into Europe from Miami.'

*Fuck me!* I thought but managed to keep a poker face.

The girls were away for about 30 minutes, so this next conversation happened in 10 minutes, more or less.

'Yeah. It can be done,' I said while thinking what to say next.

A few moments later I added, 'Obviously, depends on a few things, but yeah it's a goer.'

Bill had been quiet since I arrived back at the table. It made me jump a little when he spoke. He broke out from his taciturn shell by drawling on about how he was connected. And how he was talking to the top echelon of the Cartel. Of course, he was referring to the drugs gangs of South America. They were some of the most notorious and violent drug gangs in existence. I started to feel a little nervous at this point. My earlier lower regions excitement, the thrill provoked by my newfound female companion, was subsiding. She was now secondary.

Bill ceased talking just like he started. No warning, no intros and no endings. One minute there were words and then nothing. It was unsettling. Total silence took over the whole table. Few people can deal with a silence that goes on for longer than a few seconds. It feels uncomfortable. Many stupid people feel an urgent need to fill the verbal vacuum, often with crap. This was not an occasion to become a stupid person.

All kinds of thoughts started to rush around in my head. In the situation Eric and I found ourselves in I was thinking: *What if this? What if that?*

No one can train about this or teach it. It's not possible to go to undercover class to learn how to cope. Calmness is inbuilt. You either have it or you don't. It's that simple. Perhaps the silence lasted for about one minute. Or longer?

During the whole time, Bill and I were staring at each other. Not in any kind of confrontational way – just staring. Eye contact held between the two of us. His grey cold eyes gave nothing away. *He has the eyes of a killer. He could be a killer. He's a gangster – part of the mob.* At that point, his mouth moved again.

'Are you guys cops?'

The question rattled around inside my brain.

This is often asked when you go undercover. If not as a question, it's put as an accusation.

The first time is the worst. *Has my cover been blown? Am I a fucking useless undercover cop? Do I look, smell and talk like a cop?* It is a test!

I reacted with aggression, 'You fucking what? Yeah, course I am and you're the fucking Pope!'

Bill laughed. That took me by surprise. I didn't think humour was part of his repertoire.

Then the killer look returned. 'If you guys are, then …'

No more words – he raised one hand next to my head. I thought about slapping it away. I decided against that and remained calm, or gave the impression of calm. The Canadian joined his forefinger and middle finger and pointed the digits at my forehead. The shape imitated a gun. The pretend gun now rested on my head. I could feel the stubby fingertips against my skin.

What followed was a simulated assassination. A double-tap from a silenced semi-automatic pistol favoured by professional hitmen the world over. A close-range execution.

I went cold when I saw him mouth the silenced spitting sound. Twice, as two imaginary shells splattered my brains out of the gaping exit wounds at the far side of my head.

*Pop. Pop.*

He was serious. I believe to this day he could have been a killer.

By sheer serendipity, the girls returned to our table before I could enact any reaction to his threat. The conversation turned to the humdrum. It was quite surreal. I cannot recall what the humdrum was about. Whatever it was, it was mundane and paled into insignificance compared to the recent event. I was preoccupied. In truth, I felt like beating the shit out of him but instead decided to act cool. We all had another couple of drinks each and the mood was convivial. I faked it. We left the She Club about 2 am and hailed a taxi to a deserted illegal drinking den. There we carried on drinking until about 6 am. They served food so the night was finished off by all six of us eating a meal. The mood remained cordial throughout.

My newfound female companion returned to the hotel with me and stayed. We did not sleep until about 7.30 in the morning as we took plenty of time getting to know each other well! I woke up about 11 am on the same day and found my bed empty. She had gone. I showered and looked in the mirror as my back felt painful. She had left her mark, literally. I had scratches running down both sides of my back from my shoulders to my waist.

Two unforgettable things in one night! Perhaps three? I recall I also danced barefooted!

All four of us – Eric, Blue, Bill and I – left the Feathers and Liverpool together.

**FIFTEEN**

# THE GUN

It is a long drive from Liverpool to Mid Wales. Wales is a small country and has a long coastline. There are mountains between the coast and the Welsh–English borders. Those mountains prevent easy road access to anywhere in the middle of Wales. The four of us crammed into the van for the arduous journey. Shoulder to shoulder is an understatement.

This was going to be a trip lasting several hours in the company of two major drug dealers, one of whom was also a gangster. Yet, my main concern was my hangover. Despite the jaded feelings in body and mind, I knuckled down and concentrated.

Those hours in the van and the occasional pit stop gave Bill ample opportunity to talk or shut up. He talked and, if anything, his tone was more serious than the previous night.

With a stony face he said, 'Guys, this is serious shit. I need a new market and this country is it. You have the Rolling Stones, Beatles, Eric Clapton, Keith Richards – all those guys are serious coke heads. They need quality powder and I am Mister Quality. I need good people like you two and Blue to set up the British connection.'

Eric concentrated on driving. I nodded along in tune with Bill's plan but did not speak.

Blue broke the silence, 'No problem.'

Another silence.

Blue added, 'The south of France too.'

'Excuse me!' Bill went red in the face and I could see that he had puffed out his cheeks.

'Bill, it's the jet-set scene there. Millionaires, big yachts – the whole scene. Like a French Miami. We gotta get our cocaine into there too.'

Bill punched the faded roof lining.

'Fuck me! You nearly made me crash,' shouted Eric.

Bill raised his voice, directed at Blue, 'No way! You don't take on more than one place at a time. If you get caught you only get caught in one place, not three or four! What have I told you before? You are not listening!' Bill was the teacher and Blue the student.

Bill's outburst spelt out an abrupt end to the discussion about a new market in the south of France. Bill calmed down and started talking again about ten minutes later. Those ten minutes were uncomfortable. Bill had reinforced my thoughts of him being capable of murder.

'I got the source. No one ever forgets that. Without me and Bolivia there is no coke. I can put my hands on 50-pound weight immediately. Today. One phone call,' Bill said.

'I'm talking $24,000 for one pound. I need to know if you guys can do it.' He carried on outlining the plan.

'A pressed pound weight is no bigger than the average-sized wallet. It's easier to ship that way, less chance of detection. It's easily hidden. What I need to know is, can you guys do it?'

But he was in full flow now. He did not pause for an answer.

'These are some of the basic rules. No rip-offs, period. Your cut is what you sell it for. My advice is, don't sell less than half-weights. That way you're not getting close to the street punks. You start at 24 for one shipment of one weight. Three weights is 23. Five or more is 21, maybe 20. Okay?'

'Okay,' I said nodding comprehensively as if this was an everyday occurrence.

'If you don't have that kind of bread, find someone who has. But tell him the price per pound and a discount for quantity ... This is pure snow when it leaves me, you can cut it and cut it and cut it. When you buy off me it's not like buying the shit off the street. Oh, and payment always in greenbacks ($US).'

There was no shutting Bill up. He was on a high.

• • •

We stopped to stretch our cramped legs, take a leak and get a gulp of fresh air. The pit stop was at a roadside pub. My hangover was still hanging over me. I gulped down three swift pints of beer mixed with lemonade. Aah! I felt better.

This was as good as it gets in undercover work. We were

now Jackson and Walker, the dealers. The strange thing was that I wasn't excited. That is a good thing. It doesn't pay to show your feelings when undercover. Besides, I did not feel like a cop. I was Steve Jackson, a wild, irresponsible man prepared to break laws if it suited me. The lack of excitement came naturally to me. A police supervisor's report once recorded that if I were any more laid back, I would be horizontal! Eric was equally as cool. He acted with total indifference to events during our pit stop break.

Bill, Blue, Eric and I climbed back into the van. The plan was to drop off Blue and Bill near Lampeter so they could collect a rental car. Blue knew a farmer who rented out cars for hire. Before we set off again, Bill asked Blue how much he needed for the rental.

'About £20, I guess,' Blue responded.

Bill reached down to the floor of the van and lifted his expensive-looking attaché case to his lap. He fiddled with the combination lock until the clasps clicked open. I was astonished at the contents. There were bundles of £20 notes, about one-inch thick, fastened with a rubber band. There were about ten identical bundles. It must have totalled somewhere in the region of £10,000. That was a lot of bread! Something else caught my attention. It lay at the bottom of the case under some documents and folded shirts. It was the unmistakable blue-grey colour of a protruding pistol barrel. I became a little inwardly nervous and thought about last night's performance with the imaginary pistol.

The rest of the journey mainly consisted of Bill talking. Eric and I listened and carefully made mental notes. Those mental notes ended up as a narrative in the Llanddewi Brefi Log.

He explained the background to his operation. It was a one-man gig in Bolivia but he was helped out by two buddies. He always dealt with the same man in Bolivia and spoke with him directly. The Bolivian was not the cocoa leaf farmer. He bought the leaf and cooked it so it ended up as 100 per cent pure cocaine product. That was what Bill was buying. He was using five couriers to bring the product into the States and Canada. One was a former air hostess. Customs in Montreal knew her well and waved her through with a smile and a perfunctory 'Hi, Dawn.' Bill used a bank in the Cayman Islands to launder his drugs cash and reckoned his profits were $64,000 per month.

He also sold himself as a promoter or fixer. He was a man with connections, boasting that with two phone calls he turned over one deal involving heroin worth $1,000,000 in the States. He never saw or went near the smack. Bill trusted us. He started to push hard for us to find a money backer but cut us some slack.

'There is no rush. I'll be around for the next two weeks,' Bill drawled. 'You can get hold of me through Blue or the number I gave you,' he added.

During the journey, Bill had written down a Bristol address and telephone number. He gave it to us as his contact details while he was in the UK. Not content with a huge plot to import coke into Britain, Bill revisited the issue of dealing in stolen jewellery. But this time he extended his unlawful activities into diamond smuggling and porn. He was keen to extend his theatre of operations by recruiting the two of us.

We eventually arrived at Blue's home in Silian. It was a quick stop so Blue could assure Lily all was fine. Blue and Bill collected their rented yellow Ford Cortina from the farmer in Abermeurig, near Lampeter.

I sighed with relief when we reached the farm. It had been a long day. I was ready to say our farewells to Bill before they set off for Bristol. That pleasant English city was to be an overnight stop for them prior to scouring the south coast marinas for a fast motorboat. Bill wanted to stay at the Holiday Inn. I guess because it would be a welcome change from the seediness of the Feathers in Liverpool. And a well-travelled Canadian would know what to expect from a Holiday Inn whether it was in Bristol, Boston, Bangkok or Bolivia.

I shuddered a little when Bill announced they would follow us to Bristol. We had earlier told them that was our planned destination after we had arrived back in Wales. That was looking like a mistake. It concerned me.

Before the van and the rental car set off, Bill spoke to Eric and me, 'Remember, you know how to get hold of me, either through that number or Blue.'

Eric, nodding, said, 'It may take longer than two weeks.'

## FIFTEEN

'When you are good and ready,' came Bill's cool reply.

Bill then walked over to my side of the van. As he approached me, he was stressing that we must find the man and as quickly as we could. I assured him we would talk to the right people. He wanted a swift yes or no.

We led the way. After all, it was a route we knew blindfolded. As Eric drove, we signed to each other using our hands and whispered. We both had the same thought. Eric and I agreed not to discuss anything in the van. We were seriously thinking that Bill may have left a bug behind. We were paranoid! The M32 is a short spur of motorway that leaves the M4 Bristol to London motorway. It connects Bristol city centre with the M4. At the Bristol end of the M32, the motorway changes into a regular main road. We pulled over in a layby and they pulled in behind us.

Eric gave them directions to the Holiday Inn, Bristol and, much to our relief, they drove off toward the city centre. The normal route to Eric's home would have taken us about ten minutes. We drove for the next forty-five minutes all over Bristol. We adopted every single counter-surveillance tactic we could think of. Whatever Graham Barnard had taught us during surveillance training, we deployed a countermove. One move resulted in some damage to the van. Eric pulled a handbrake U-turn. The chainsaw in the back of the van ricocheted about from one side to the other putting a dent in the bare metal van walls.

Finally, we were content we were not being followed.

We both blew a simultaneous sigh of relief and exclaimed, 'Fuck me!'

. . .

This encounter warranted a special journey into Devizes to brief Dick Lee and make a full record of the whole episode. We did just that the next day. Our report to Lee was exact. It also included we had learned that Bill had a Canadian passport, a British wife and two kids residing in the Isle of Man. It was believed that his net worth was about $3,000,000 despite some Canadian tax problems. But Bill did say he wasn't sure about the exact amount as "he hadn't counted it lately!"

Eric and I recounted the Liverpool events to Lee with relish. I had never seen Dick Lee stay so quiet for so long.

He stood open-mouthed as we told him the story.

When we had finished, he slumped into his office chair and exclaimed, 'Fuck me!'

Eric laughed and said, 'That's what we said.'

I couldn't resist adding, 'Guv, is that an official: "fuck me" or just an ordinary "fuck me"?'

Lee had the last word: 'Smart arse. It's a you-have-given-me-a-problem "fuck me", so fuck off!' His face had come alive thinking of the magnitude of our tale.

Eric and I left Lee's office holding our sides to ease the pain of laughing. Martyn Pritchard was also in the squad office that day. It was rare to see all three undercover guys in the office at the same time[10].

Martyn saw us doubled up with laughter as we came out through the door of Lee's office.

'Hey man! What's with the giggles?' Martyn asked.

Eric and I laughed even more. We never knew if Martyn was really a head or just talked like one. We took him to one side and told him the same story we had just related to Lee.

'Fuck me!' Martyn said, maybe he added, 'far out, man.'

## SIXTEEN

## IDIOT!

We had already found out that Cartref was available for rent. It was a small, stone terrace, two-bedroom cottage close to the centre of Llanddewi Brefi. Pam owned it. She was the ex of John Mayall, a well-known British blues artist. We agreed to a rental of £10 weekly and we moved into our new home on 7 September 1976. That was another expense for Peter Long to worry about.

Pam was an attractive woman. We soon ran out of excuses to go see her at her large home outside the village on the way to Lampeter. There was another valid reason why we stopped thinking of excuses to gaze on her beauty. The last time we saw her she had a visitor. He was a Welsh police officer from the local force. He was a smarmy type to whom I took an instant dislike. I distrusted him. Welsh people, maybe more so than others, seem to have an insatiable curiosity. That, with the fact he was paid to be curious as a police officer, gave me a bad feeling about him.

We never returned to see Pam at her house again. I always had some misgivings about Welsh officers forming part of Operation Julie. Not so much members of the South Wales Police based in Cardiff, but the local Dyfed-Powys

Police. Dyfed-Powys was then a police area responsible for the two counties of Dyfed and Powys. It was largely a rural area with mountains in the centre and coastal plains. These rural areas are sparsely populated. The people who do live there know everybody else and their business. Police officers are no exception to the general rule that people gossip. On top of that, there was the existence of freemasonry.

Many police services in England and Wales were riddled with freemasonry. I am sure the Dyfed-Powys force was no different. Freemasonry is secretive by nature. Freemasonry observers will often tell you that there is a promotion ladder – a direct link between police officer freemasons and promotion. It was all a combination with which I felt ill at ease.

Dick Lee may have had the same thoughts when persuading the Home Office and the Association of Chief Police Officers (ACPO) to set up Operation Julie. If he did, then I feel he compromised to get his baby up and running. Ultimately, I found the Dyfed-Powys officers on Operation Julie to be honourable men. I would, even now, trust them with my life. Perhaps Lee's mantra of hand-picking the men and women was correct. He chose officers with integrity. We erred on the side of caution to protect our cover. Eric and I did ask members of the Operation Julie squad not to use Lampeter police station under any circumstances because that was the base for Pam's pet officer.

* * *

The New Inn became even more of a feature in our routine now that we had moved into our cottage in Llanddewi Brefi. It was close and convenient. No sooner had we moved into the cottage than the wheels threatened to fall off in our undercover world. The internal politics I alluded to earlier had one by-product. We seemed to have a new boss.

He was Detective Superintendent Dennis Greenslade, an Avon and Somerset detective. He had been drafted in from the Bristol-based Regional Crime Squad. Greenslade had always been the executive commander with Dick Lee as the operational commander. But the Super was a boss in name only. Few appeared to like or respect him, partly because of who he was as a man and partly because the squad had an unwavering belief in Dick Lee and total allegiance to him.

I held the opinion that Greenslade was a spy and a puppet. Although a boss, he also had bosses. His bosses were ACPO and the Home Office. He wasted no time in poking into what we were doing in Llanddewi Brefi. On one of our daily phone-ins, Greenslade told us he wanted us to install a VHF radio in the cottage so we could use it as a new reporting method. The convenience of mobile phones did not exist in 1976. Our reaction was one of incredulity.

The following day things got clearer. We were told over the phone that Greenslade had made it clear the issue of the VHF radio was not an option. It was not a request but an order. I was furious. The rest of that day we spread about a story to cover our absence for a day or two. The next day we drove in through the gates of Devizes HQ in Eric's own car. We left the van in Bristol per our usual practice.

Eric and I were in a buoyant and confident mood. This was soon after our dealings with Bill in Liverpool. I believed we were in a position of strength. Position of strength or not, there were to be no negotiations. No discussions with Greenslade about the installation of a VHF radio set in Cartref, our new home. This detective was not for budging one inch.

'Where's Greenslade?' Everyone in the room heard me.

An unfamiliar voice squeaked, 'Mister Greenslade, or Sir, to you.'

It was an answer guaranteed to raise my hackles even more. I saw the source of the voice in a separate office next to Dick Lee's office. I spotted Lee. He looked at me with that familiar grin and moved both his hands in unison. First over his eyes, then ears and finally mouth. I didn't need any encouragement from this 'three wise monkeys routine.' Lee was indicating that he was not a witness to what was to follow.

Greenslade looked old, tall, pale and insignificant. A loose-fitting and tasteless suit covered his lean limbs. He was no snappy dresser. I walked toward him dressed in dirty denim and worn-out sneakers. I wore my dirty woollen hat. My hair was by now long and unkempt. My beard was full and my face tanned. He did not impress me. Goodness knows what he thought about me and my appearance.

I sensed no charisma, no leadership. He spoke again and that confirmed what I was thinking about him. He had a thin, reedy voice and a strong West Country burr. It was a voice that failed to command respect or attention and carried no tone of authority.

'I take it you are Bentley.'

'DC Bentley, or Steve, to you.'

'No need to be cheeky.'

'I'm not.'

'Alright then, what do you want to see me about?'

'This stupid plan of yours to stick a VHF radio in the cottage.'

'It's not a plan. You must have the radio to keep in touch so we know you are both okay.'

Sarcasm dictated my response.

'Thanks for thinking about our welfare but we've been fine until you stepped in.'

His face turned puce, 'Look, I told you – don't be insubordinate!'

'It's not happening.'

'What isn't?'

'Radio, cottage – cottage, radio. It's not gonna happen!'

I swear he hovered a few inches off the ground. His arms were crooked and flapped by his side as if in a synchronised dance. He looked like a demented giant rooster.

He calmed down and returned to earth.

'Are you refusing to install a VHF radio in your cottage?'

'You finally got the message, right?'

'You do realise that this could mean a disciplinary charge?'

'Yes, and I hope you realise that by sticking a bloody VHF radio in there you are facing a potential charge of endangering two undercover officers under your command?'

'What do you mean?'

'What? You don't really know? Let me spell it out – VHF bandwidth is not secure. Anyone can listen in. We wouldn't have a clue who could be listening to our conversations with the office.'

'What do you think, DC Wright?' Greenslade turned to Eric who was stood by the office door.

Eric did a twirling motion with his finger pointing to his head and spoke one word. 'Idiot!'

We turned and left the office. We vowed never to speak with Greenslade again during the operation.

That night I stayed at Eric's before we returned to Wales the next day. After a meal and a few whiskies, later we burst out laughing.

'"Idiot" – is that all you could think of?'

We roared!

• • •

Greenslade had to try and have the last word and leave his stamp of authority. About a week later, we met Vince Castle, a DS on the Julie squad, on our way back to Llanddewi Brefi. Vince was acting as a peacemaker. I always respected him so I listened. He handed us a VHF radio set. It seemed to me that Vince was in an unenviable position. He was carrying out his orders from Greenslade but he also appeared to empathise with our stance on the issue of the VHF radio.

We agreed to take it with us but only for the sake of Vince. I wasn't interested in placating Greenslade at all. I'm not saying Eric was. He wasn't the type to placate idiots. On arrival at the cottage, Eric carried in the VHF radio set. Carried undercover, of course; under wraps, anyway. He decided to hide it away in the loft. A small trap door at the top of the stairs gave access to the loft or attic. It stayed there for a few days while we deliberated what to do about it.

Eric decided to experiment. Standing on a chair at the top of the stairs, he removed the trap door. He switched on the set and waited for a few minutes. Adopting a false Welsh accent, Eric picked up the phone-like mouthpiece. Then spoke into it. It was gibberish and didn't mean anything at all. It wasn't meant to mean anything.

Some two hours later we went to the New Inn for a pint. We had been in there for perhaps thirty minutes when we overheard a conversation in the corner of the bar. They were ordinary locals talking among themselves.

'Watch out boys. We heard some strange transmissions coming over the radio earlier tonight.'

It was unmistakable what they were discussing both in Welsh and English. They were referring to Eric's garbled message. We had warned Greenslade that locals could hear any transmissions, and we were right.

Eric and I walked the short journey back to the cottage. Eric clambered up onto the chair once more. I thought for one moment he was going to make another transmission. Then I saw the screwdriver in his hand. Suddenly, the set refused to work! We took it back to Devizes on our next visit.

'Sorry boss, the radio's broke,' Eric said as he dropped it onto a table in front of Greenslade.

Eric used a technical term to me to describe what he had done: 'I've fucked it up good and proper, mate!'

We later discovered that there had been a Royal visit to Wales. This was at the same time Eric tried his test transmission. The locals attributed Eric's strange transmission to that event. That was a relief to both of us. We both hated that radio and the thought of it being in the cottage. It's a wonder one of us didn't stick it in a part of Greenslade's anatomy the sun didn't reach!

That wasn't the only occasion that the idea of sticking an inanimate object up Greenslade's inner recesses struck either of us.

• • •

A West Country hotel was the scene for a final post-Operation Julie reunion dinner. It had been arranged for the squad personnel after the sentencing of the conspirators. Eric bumped into Greenslade in a corridor of the hotel. Greenslade paced around in circles with a puzzled frown on his face while holding a plaque. He had been asked to present it to one of the squad members.

He spotted Eric and said, 'Where do you think I should put this, Eric?'

'Sir, you really don't want to know the answer to that!'

That brief exchange was the only conversation Eric, or I, held with Greenslade since the VHF radio incident, save for one.

The months wore on in our undercover role in such a small community so we toyed with the idea of having some female company. This seemed to us to be a good idea on two fronts. One, it gave us an air of normality. Two, there were a few occasions when Eric or I were not available. For example, both Eric and I both took a period of holiday leave at different times. We became close, but not so close that we holidayed together!

In any case, we both had pre-booked holidays paid in full, and we didn't want to lose our money. Our respective families needed a break too. Both of us discussed the idea of bringing along a woman to go with us for a few days in Llanddewi Brefi. We discounted the notion of bringing one of the Operation Julie policewomen. To use Eric's words at the time, 'They looked, smelled and spoke like policewomen'. Sorry ladies, no disrespect, but it was true.

Eric broached this subject with Greenslade. He insisted on Eric taking along one of our female squad officers. Eric refused to do that and repeated that they looked, smelled, and talked like policewomen. That bemused Greenslade. He could not understand the import of Eric's wise words. What's more, he forbade Eric to take Jan. If there was ever a woman who could pull this off, it had to be Jan. She was smart, cool and could fit in with ease. She even hand-rolled her own cigarettes! She also had the bonus of being attractive – more than could be said for some of the policewomen.

Eric was reluctant but decided to go behind Greenslade's back. He decided to ambush Ken Steele, Eric's Chief Constable (CC) of the Avon and Somerset Constabulary. Eric pounced one early morning in the car park at his force HQ. Mr Steele seemed initially shocked at the idea but listened with close attention to what Eric had to say. In the end, he saw the force in Eric's argument and agreed. Greenslade was furious and didn't speak to either of us again until the reunion dinner at the hotel.

Eric and Jan spent a few days together in Llanddewi Brefi. It helped in an immeasurable way in fostering our cover. It helped even more when they left photos laying around our cottage. Photos showing the mountain regions of Morocco. Eric and Jan had been there on holiday a short time earlier. It was the subject of conversations with Smiles, Buzz and Blue. It is the little things that can make a difference. They can make the subterfuge work. We also arranged to address letters to ourselves at the cottage. Letters that once more we left around in case a visitor read them. They contained subtle references to drugs, prices and dealing.

Jan met Smiles and Buzz in Wales. Eric, Jan, Smiles and Buzz were having a drink together in a Tregaron pub. The presence of Jan helped Smiles accept that we were who we said we were. But Smiles being Smiles, he could not help pressing buttons one more time. He again made a reference to Reagan and Carter. Eric and Jan both ignored the comment. Eric bided his time. He waited until Jan needed to use the WC. Eric asked Smiles to go to the back of the pub as he needed a word with him in private. He went through a charade. Eric told Smiles not to mention coppers ever again, particularly if I was present. To reinforce his point, Eric raised his fist.

Smiles cried, 'Not the teeth, please not the teeth!'

The problem with police officers like Greenslade is a lack of brain capacity. They have a total lack of flexibility in attitudes and tactics. For every good leader, I guess there must be several idiots. We had an idiot as a nominal leader. A leader in name only. And I'm not talking about Dick Lee.

## SEVENTEEN

# STEVE AND ERIC
# – DEALERS

### 8 September 1976

Now high on the action and adrenaline flowing – the incident in Liverpool was exciting in the extreme. We had impressed Lee with our work there. We equally impressed him in the small details we recalled and committed to paper in our report. But it presented a conundrum of our making.

On one hand, he was reluctant to let the cocaine plot distract us or him from the LSD investigation. On the other, it was a huge opportunity. A chance to take out what appeared to be a big player in the cocaine business. One with direct links to South America. Lee instructed us to keep Blue on a string, to encourage him but not to commit to anything. We were to play for time. Bill concerned me, not Blue. Bill was a serious player and not one to mess around. I was mindful of the double-tap episode, not to mention the gun in the attaché case. I asked Lee for Smith & Wesson .38 Detective Specials to be issued to us.

'Fuck off,' was his simple answer to my query.

We played the waiting game for all we were worth. Blue called in on us at Cartref about a week after the return from Liverpool. The talk was almost all about Bill. Blue had returned yesterday from a trip with the fellow Canadian to Bristol. He confirmed they had also visited the south coast of England and Porthcawl. It appeared that Bill had located a boat and was going to pay £30,000 for it.

Blue was keen to progress with the cocaine venture. He talked about a deal involving Bill in Canada for $3 million worth of heroin. The deal went sour when two guys were busted in Vancouver and were now serving 12 years in jail. A group of professionals in Vancouver, such as lawyers and doctors, were the source of the buy money. The impression given was that Bill was the fixer, never going near the product.

This impromptu visit by Blue gave force to our refusal to install a VHF radio in Cartref. Blue visited us at the cottage many times. Sometimes Lily, his lady, accompanied him.

Cartref was a small cottage with nowhere to hide a VHF radio set other than in the loft. And that wasn't foolproof. Greenslade really didn't have a clue! The cottage did not afford us much privacy. I am comparing it to using the van as our home. We had unscheduled visits at the cottage. Visits from Blue, sometimes with Lily. From time to time, Happy also called in on us at Cartref.

## September 13

Five days later we paid Blue a visit at his home. Lily disappeared after making tea for the three of us. She knew we were going to discuss business.

A large solid oak table dominated the main room of the house. It had six spindle backed chairs. Drawing up our chairs, I spoke first.

'We saw our man a few days ago. Put him in the picture about the snow and he's interested but he needs time to put the bread together.'

'That's cool. You sure he's serious?'

'Deadly. He wants to take all we can bring in. That's why he needs time.'

'Good. I'd rather us deal through one here than a few. Less risk. I've spoken to Bill and told him no need to rush.'

Blue explained he would prefer to deal in 5lb weights but even 1lb at a time would be fine. He would even consider half-pound weights. He went on talking about the high grade of this Bolivian cocaine and emphasised the market for it among the rich and famous. Just like before, he dropped names of members of the Rolling Stones and other bands.

'We need to keep Bill isolated. There's no need to meet him again until we throw a party to celebrate the first consignment. I'm the man between you two and Bill. I don't want to meet your man, that's your affair.'

Eric came in, 'How will we get hold of the product?'

'Good question, Ginger. Bill's couriers will bring it in, right. You don't need to know how I get it. I will drop it and hide it somewhere no one will ever stumble across it, like a remote forest. You then go retrieve it.'

'What about payment?' I asked.

'Okay, here's what happens. I arrange to meet you in a hotel – London, Manchester or somewhere. I will book the rooms. You just need to turn up.'

'Right, but how do we find you at the hotel?' I queried.

'You will be told which room I have booked you into. Just check in and go to your room. I'll leave a message in that room to tell you to come to my room. I will watch your room to make sure there is no fuss.'

'This better be level. Fuck me, we are sitting ducks with loads of bread in our sky.' (skyrocket is rhyming slang for pocket.)

'Steve, Steve – do you trust me?'

'Course I fucking trust you. I wouldn't be here if I didn't trust you.'

Blue beamed and said, 'Fucking A!'

All three of us shook hands and clinked the tea mugs together in a toast to riches!

The conversation then turned to Smiles. Blue touted him as a possible alternative if our man blew out. We poured scorn on that idea by saying he was too paranoid. Blue agreed but added that his contacts could be useful as a last resort. Before we left, Blue was the first in our conspiracy to convert weight prices into sterling. He said a pound of cocaine was £12,000. Of course, this was the high-grade stuff and would be cut time and time again as it travelled down the distribution chain.

Blue liked the cut of our cloth. He liked us and the truth is, we liked him. All three of us gelled. Even knowing we were playing a part in a charade, I had believed in my new persona. When does acting become living the part? I started to dream about luxury cars and villas in the sun! It was also gratifying to know that he trusted us one hundred per cent.

A big part of my belief in the charade was the unswerving support we received from Dick Lee and others at Devizes. Support by the Devizes team for this visit to Blue enhanced our credibility one thousand per cent.

As we were leaving Blue's home, Eric said in the most nonchalant way, 'Look we can't stop. We are on a run. Come take a look in the back of the van.'

He did as Eric suggested. Blue's eyes opened wide at what he saw after we had removed the cover of the false bottom of a large tool chest. He saw thirteen weights of black (high-grade Lebanese hash) stacked in the false compartment. Next to it lay a sawn-off shotgun.

We had him hook, line and sinker!

The hash and the shotgun were later returned to the Bristol Drugs Store.

Life carried on after these high days of adrenaline rush. We felt fireproof but not in a rash or reckless way. We were never overconfident. Wheels can always drop off! Especially when least expected.

Our usual intelligence activities continued unabated – listening and watching. Noting car licence plate numbers and reporting daily to Devizes. Using a secluded telephone kiosk, not a VHF radio set. We bumped into Happy again and he intimated that Smiles was into acid in a big way. There was no urge to tell him we knew that already.

The September days had now drifted into October. We turned the heater on in the van for the first time and it worked. The memories of the summer heatwave were fast vanishing. More is the pity, as I so enjoyed the rock pool and the solitude of the mountains. We were now a part of the fabric of the village and surrounding area. A head we had met early on in our days here, the Scots guy, told us he could get rid of a weight a week if we came up with the goods. He was busted as a side product of the Julie busts in a relatively minor case of importing cannabis into the UK. He served 12 months in prison.

October passed and it was now November 1976. There was no end in sight to the Operation Julie investigation, although all on the squad were acutely aware of the political pressure to wrap it up. Lee was a stubborn and dogged individual. He got more time, owing to his tenacity and determination.

We received more time, too. We always updated Lee on developments with Blue and Bill. We reported anything new about the plot to import large consignments of cocaine. We carried out our instructions from Lee to the letter. It was 3 November 1976, when we had a further conversation with Blue about cocaine. Eric and I told him that our man could not come up with the money. It wasn't a problem with Blue. He shrugged and was content to wait for us to come back to him with some positive news.

An entry in the Llanddewi Brefi Log on 9 November 1976, still amuses me when reading it years later:

> *Approached while at the Red Lion by a local kid called [name deleted] about dealing dope. He seemed to have the idea we were dope dealers.*

I wonder how he gained that impression?

The Scots guy, together with Eric and I, had a few drinks with a group of heads in the Red Lion, Tregaron. We were also shooting pool. I had become proficient on the pool table and was now the self-appointed pool king of Wales. Another head called Thomas joined our company.

Jock, the Scot, asked Thomas if he still had the half-kilo of Nepalese. He hadn't, as he said he had got rid of it, meaning he'd sold it all.

Thomas was most enlightening on how he brought his contraband into the country. He explained in some detail how he and three others brought in 55lbs of hashish. They flew out and back on separate flights. He described the route as:

- London–Nepal
- Nepal–Trans-Siberian Railway to Moscow
- Moscow–East Berlin (via plane)
- East Berlin–Leipzig (via bus or train)
- Leipzig–London (via plane)

Someone would then meet them near Heathrow airport where the final transactions took place. Our new loquacious friend also added he was taking advance orders for the next trip.

• • •

The following day we went out as usual. On our return, there was a note from Blue stuck under the front door. He wanted to talk about business. There was no rush to follow up on this message.

The New Inn was once more the venue for another friendly meeting with Smiles. It was lunchtime the day after we had got the note from Blue. Smiles made a point of telling us he had spoken with Blue. He knew about the proposed cocaine venture and revealed that Blue had spoken to him in some detail about it and was aware of our part. Smiles was circumspect. The conversation soon turned to other mundane matters. Was Smiles now convinced by us? I wasn't sure just yet. That perception of mine was about to change. It was a dramatic change over the course of the next few weeks and months.

## EIGHTEEN

# DOUG

Market day in Tregaron is every Tuesday. Tuesday, 16 November 1976, was no different except it was also the annual fair day. Tregaron is the hub of local activity, especially on market days. This was especially so for the locals, Welsh and heads alike, involved in farming or livestock. There is an auction on market day. Farmers could sell and bid for animals, particularly cattle, sheep and horses. Eric, being the country boy, dragged me there one day and I must admit it was a fascinating experience.

He taught me about a breed of cattle known as Charolais. I used to mispronounce it as 'Chevrolet' on purpose. It was my way of spelling out to Eric that I was the city boy. Fair Day was an annual event that dated back to an ancient November tradition. It owed its origins to the days when labourers converged on the market from the surrounding hills. They would negotiate with land and farm owners over new terms – their new reward for sweat in the fields and cattle sheds.

Smiles, Buzz, Happy, Eric and I were drinking all day long that day in Tregaron. The pubs were open all day owing to the fair. They didn't close for the normal afternoon break imposed by the liquor licensing laws prevailing at that time.

It was a marathon session. Smiles was on top form and was his usual extrovert self. He was an extrovert, but never boastful. A man who enjoyed life and was not afraid to show it. Buzz and Happy were mere followers, quite content to bask in the popularity zone that was the signature of Smiles. This was a man who could have been a TV or movie star, such was his charisma and good looks. He was generous, too. This was no doubt one of the reasons why the likes of Buzz and Happy stuck to him like metal filings attracted to a magnet. There were stories that Smiles had once lit a big fat cigar using a £20 note he pulled from his wallet and ignited. We never did witness such largesse on his part but it would not surprise me if that story was true.

Another man was in our heavy-drinking company that day. We had never met him before. His name was Doug.

A clear picture had fallen into place. A picture of the distribution network of Todd/Cuthbertson, Fielding, Spenceley and Smiles. The picture was the result of a combination of regular detective work, surveillance, telephone intercepts and the undercover work carried out by Pritchard in Wiltshire and by us in Wales. There was still intense pressure on Lee to bring the curtain down on the show but Lee stuck to his guns. He was right, as in November 1976 we were not sure where the acid-manufacturing laboratory was. Or indeed, if it was in full swing or now under wraps ready for the next run. In any event, the theory of two labs was gaining momentum.

# EIGHTEEN

The telephone intercept on Smiles's home revealed the existence of Doug. It was clear Smiles was supplying acid to him in considerable quantities. In turn, Doug was supplying it to street-level dealers in London. Nothing much else was known of Doug. Lee asked us to make the identification of him a priority. This was particularly the case as the telephone tap on Smiles had revealed a man called Tony. He was later identified as Tony Dalton. Dalton had arranged to meet Doug at a London pub. Frustration overcame Lee. There was insufficient time to put together a surveillance team to cover this meeting.

My tolerance level to alcohol had increased week by week, month by month. I suppose it was normal when we had first entered the village of Llanddewi Brefi in June. I was now able to drink vast amounts without falling over in a drunken stupor. My brain was always alert even if my body or legs stuttered and wobbled. This was a great attribute to have as an undercover officer. It proved priceless on this day.

It was a good day. Six guys all having fun in the pub. Between Smiles, Eric and me, we must have bought ninety per cent of the drinks consumed that day. Doug seemed to feel the effects of the alcohol first among our company. He didn't appear drunk at first, just silly. Doug and Smiles knew each other well. It was clear to me that this Doug was the one that Lee needed us to identify. It helped matters that Doug liked us and trusted us. He wrote down his telephone number on a piece of paper and handed it to Eric. That was a good start, but it still did not identify him.

By 'identifying him', I mean finding out exactly who he is. We needed his full name, date of birth, address and criminal convictions (if any). We needed to know his associates. In my own mind, this was *the* Doug. We had to devise a method to identify him without breaking or even jeopardising our cover story – no easy task.

Message to the brain – keep working, keep functioning, you need to do your job. This was my method of stopping my brain from falling into the abyss of alcohol-induced abandonment of reasoning and function. An abandonment of caring about who I was supposed to be.

This concentration took the form of an alarm clock, an imaginary constant clanging clockwork contraption lodged inside my head, with two huge mechanical bells set symmetrically on top. It worked for me not only this night but on other nights too. Times when the source of the intoxicant was not only alcohol but also tetrahydrocannabinol (THC – the active ingredient of cannabis) and benzoylmethylecgonine (cocaine).

Smiles, Buzz and Happy took their leave of the drunken company. That was a sensible move. Doug was drunk. We bought him another couple of beers and shots to ensure he stayed that way. I had a wicked plan tucked away up my sleeve.

Slurring by now, I said, 'Doug, where are you staying tonight?'

My brain was functioning fine. But the words coming out from my mouth bore a resemblance to Donald Duck.

'Smiles's,' Doug indicated.

'Right, we'll give you a lift,' I slurred.

All three of us left the pub in Tregaron stumbling down the stone steps leading to the high street. The van was parked about 50 yards distant. As we walked past some shops toward, the van I noticed two things. Doug was swerving from side to side. A few steps forward, a few back. His legs buckled as he tried to walk. He was gone! The other thing I noticed was the street had emptied.

The time was ripe to roll out my plan. It was easy for me to act almost as drunk as Doug because I was almost as drunk as Doug. Yet, my next moves were purely voluntary. I controlled my limbs long enough to overcome my drunkenness. Doug was on the inside with me next to him. Using the outside of my hip of my right leg, I thrust it rapidly into his left leg. It was a trick I had learned from playing in countless football games. It is a subtle and effective way of unbalancing an opponent.

The flick of the hip sent him crashing back through the shop window. There was an almighty sound of glass crashing, freed from its captivity as a rigid form. Doug lay inside the shop, stranded like an upturned turtle. It took me a few moments to assess the scene. Relief took over when I could see no blood. His chest was rising and falling with that human reflex action indicative of life itself.

The task was not yet completed. I was about to execute the second part of the wicked plan. It was late at night. The earlier streams of people, who had congregated for market and fair day, had petered out. I could not guarantee that the local police would find the drunken Doug and the smashed shop window. Several yards away stood one of the ubiquitous red phone boxes, or telephone kiosks – 'TKs' as we called them in police lingo. I dialled 999 and got through to the operator.

'Which service do you require?'

'Police.'

The Llanddewi Brefi Log entry for Wednesday, 17 November 1976, read:

*Doug was busted by the local law last night for smashing a window and* [being] *drunk and disorderly.*

Job done! *The* Doug was now identified as Douglas John Flanagan.

• • •

We left the scene after the 999 call and drove toward our cottage in Llanddewi Brefi. It's about four miles. We could only make it halfway. I was driving and my brain short-circuited – my inbuilt alarm clock system gave up for the day. I needed sleep. I pulled over into what I thought was a layby. It was now about 12.30am. The noise of trucks and horns beeping woke us at about eight o'clock in the morning. The van was not in a layby but parked on the narrow main road with the back end sticking out toward the centre line.

With the benefit of hindsight, the Doug incident was a reckless thing to do. It could have backfired and Doug could have been seriously injured, or worse. Those were crazy days and this was one more example of the craziness. He now has a criminal conviction that he did not deserve. Yet, I ask this – considering the circumstances and the minor nature of those charges – did the ends justify the means? I think so. We accomplished our mission. Doug was tagged and put into the system as a dealer. He was now a known-known and no longer a known-unknown. In any event, his undeserving conviction for criminal damage somewhat paled into insignificance when compared to his later conviction and sentence of imprisonment. He was one of the distributors of the LSD within the Operation Julie conspiracy.

What if Eric and I had been arrested? You may ask this question because it could have happened on any number of occasions. It was possible the DEA or the Regional Crime Squad knew about Blue and Bill. If that was the case, then maybe they recorded conversations between Blue, Bill, Eric and me. There would have been evidence to justify our arrest and questioning.

This is the answer – at no time were we to reveal to any police officer our true identities. We would have had to succumb to the normal procedures of arrest and detention, giving our false details and maintaining our cover. We had a get-out-of-jail-free card up our sleeves.

There was one other police officer who knew of our undercover role, other than those within Operation Julie. He was a high-ranking police officer, an Assistant Chief Constable and a member of ACPO. And, he was one of the few sympathetic toward Dick Lee and Operation Julie.

Both Eric and I had memorised his name and private telephone number. In the event of our arrest and detention, we had a set procedure to follow. We would have requested the arresting officer contact his senior officer. That senior officer was to contact his own Chief Constable. The Chief Constable was to telephone the number we had supplied. That Chief Constable, in turn, would have ordered our immediate release. No questions asked or answers given.

I never had confidence in the protocol. We never had to use the arrangement.

# NINETEEN

# CHILLUM

The routine was now set in stone. Our haunts were the New Inn at Llanddewi Brefi and the pubs of Tregaron. We listened, watched, and talked in that order of priority. We were now welcome regulars at the New Inn. As much a part of the furniture as the locals, Smiles or the fixtures and fittings of a typical country pub. We were having many friendly chats with Smiles. It was common for us to spend two or so hours drinking in his company. We did notice something about Smiles's habits. Even when his wife, Mary, accompanied him to the pub, it was obvious that the house was never left unattended. It was later to become clear that the reason for this was nothing to do with babysitters. It was more to do with the secrets of Y Glyn.

We were also becoming frequently invited guests of Smiles in his home. He loved his music and was keen to play me his latest tastes, which also became part of my tastes. He introduced me to Joan Armatrading and Steely Dan. I will always be grateful to him for that. He also introduced me to Buddhist meditation. He had a whole room that looked like it was a shrine dedicated to Shiva, or maybe Vishnu. I am no expert on Hindu gods or goddesses. It was de rigeur to sit cross-legged in meditation with him and chant 'Omm'. The sound repeated and uttered in a slow melody. This was irrefutable evidence that I had adopted a new persona. The meditation was often preceded by inhaling marijuana. Unlike a former President of the United States, I did inhale – big time!

It was during one of these meditation sessions I almost did the unthinkable. I was so chilled, relaxed and at peace with the world. So completely comfortable in my new skin of Steve Jackson. I was in a space where Steve Bentley, the undercover policeman, did not exist. I had grown to like Smiles. I enjoyed his company. He was fun, intelligent and good-hearted.

I knew a time would come when I would betray him. Or at least betray our friendship. Make no mistake, I was now Jackson and fully living the lie. I have read accounts by actors when they say a character role had taken over their own personality. I understand that. I was playing a role in a real-life movie, one that was never going to make it into celluloid. It was a one-take movie with no room for mistakes or fumbling lines. It was also like having a split personality. On occasions, my alter ego would perch on my shoulder to remind me who I was. I came so close to warning Smiles. I wanted to do that. It was a fight to subdue a strong urge to tell him all.

My other self, the real me, prevented me from spilling the beans. I cannot over-emphasise how strong those emotions were. No one, and I mean no one, can understand what it felt like unless they have been in that same situation. It plays with your mind. I guess it could be described as a reverse

Stockholm Syndrome. To this day, I often still feel more comfortable with the part of me that was Steve Jackson.

Mac and Buzz were as friendly as Smiles. They liked a game of cards. A game with Mac, Smiles, Eric and I happened after a drinking session in the New Inn. It was evening. We all went to Smiles's home, Y Glyn, to play. Mac produced his weed and skinned up a large joint. It was offered to me first, as an honoured guest. I was to light it and have the first go at puffing on it.

I am sure many of you are familiar with the social niceties of cannabis smoking. For those unfamiliar, this is a quick guide.

A joint is a hand-rolled cannabis cigarette. It may take the form of weed, hash or sometimes THC oil painted onto the cigarette papers. It has one end containing the roach, an improvised filter often made from a torn corner of a Rizla cigarette paper packet. The other end consists of the overhanging paper. You twist that paper to prevent the contents falling out.

I took the joint from Mac and said thanks. All eyes are now on me watching me light the joint, anticipating their turn in eagerness.

'You've lit the wrong end!' came the cries from all present, as if I had committed a grave crime.

Okay, I was drunk. That was the excuse I gave. Mac and Smiles accepted the excuse, much to their amusement and my relief. It was the only time I can say in truth I became anxious about my role because of a gaffe. I thought to myself, *How can they possibly believe who I say I am if I didn't know one end of a joint from the other?*

I did say earlier that there was no training for undercover work back in my day. Everything I did was flying by the seat of my pants. It was a mix of improvisation and intuition while also applying some common sense. That incident with Mac and lighting the wrong end could have been disastrous. It turned out just fine owing to my ability to laugh at myself, make others laugh with me and make them so relaxed that it all faded into insignificance. The fact I had become an accomplished liar also helped. I did not repeat such a stupid mistake.

I was gaining pounds around my waist owing to the regular heavy-drinking sessions. Especially during the cold, dark, and often wet winter days in the village. Every day was a booze day. Every other day was turning into a weed or hash occasion when mixing with the likes of Mac, Smiles and Buzz. We had turned into the characters we strived to portray. Our acting was successful, but would there ultimately be a price to pay?

• • •

Another card night took place in Smiles's home. Once more both Smiles and Mac were present. All smoked weed. It was accompanied by copious amounts of bourbon. Smiles produced a chillum and loaded it with hash. The burning hash pipe reached me. It was now my turn. I obliged the watching company. Maybe they thought I was going to insert the bowl end into my mouth?

Within a few minutes of finishing a second big gulp of THC-laden smoke, I felt a little queasy. My head had started to spin and I felt disoriented. It unsettled me and I began to feel uneasy. The voices from the bodies in the room became separate entities, detached from any person. I knew that those disembodied voices emanated from people in the room, but I could not figure out why the voice and the speaker had become divisible.

Voices slowed down like an old gramophone record playing at the wrong speed on a turntable. The playing cards on the table appeared huge and out of all proportion to the size of the table. The Queen of Diamonds was smiling at me! She knew my secret. This was becoming the test of tests. I recognised that I was paranoid. I was hallucinating and summoned up all my inner resolve to act in a natural way. The sick feeling in my stomach was worsening and I paid a visit to the WC. It was just a few strides away in a bathroom located on the ground floor of the house. I made it in time to throw up. It was the violent kind of retching.

The vomit was dribbling from my mouth into the bowl as I leaned on the wall using my outstretched arms. A fresh but minor eruption spewed forth and landed in the bowl of the WC. I saw a kaleidoscopic array of colours as I peered at the contents of the bowl.

From the centre of the bowl, a large dragon's head rose toward me. It was alive and got larger as it came up to meet my face. I wasn't scared. It was both eerie and fascinating. The head pulsed back and forth, shrinking and then magnifying as it neared my own face once more. I could see the scales in detail, the red eyes and fire spitting forth from its mouth. I have no idea how long this lasted. It seemed like hours. But when I unlocked the bathroom door to return to the card table, no one mentioned my absence. I was still hallucinating, but not to the same degree. It was now pleasant and once more I could relax.

The hallucinatory effects of smoking from the chillum were still active when Eric and I left. We made the short walk back to the cottage from Y Glyn. The road outside is some 15 yards wide. Terraced cottages framed the road on both sides. I walked in an unsteady fashion, my gait affected by both alcohol and the chillum. The result was one of those staggering sideways walks that is the hallmark of the drunk.

I walked sideways but still made gradual forward momentum. I developed a strange new ability. I became able to touch the walls of both rows of houses on both sides of the road. Not at the same time, but with ease. Just like I was taking one step then touch, another step in the opposite direction and touch. It was a game I was enjoying like an excited child. The road seemed to have narrowed. Narrowed in a dramatic way. The terraces were closer together.

I shouted to Eric, 'This is great. I can touch them without moving!'

'Fucking idiot,' is what I heard him say.

No one, not even Eric, was going to rain on this parade. I gazed skywards toward a clear winter sky. There were millions if not zillions of stars all twinkling and winking. I swear they were close enough to touch.

I jumped up towards them and my euphoria evaporated on my inability to reach the stars.

# TWENTY

# CHRISTMAS 1976

Blue had cooled down by mid December. We saw him from time to time but there was hardly any talk of Bill or cocaine. There were still times he came to visit us and chat for a while. On one such occasion, he left behind his wallet. That was careless of him. As a natural detective thing, we examined the contents. There was a telegram from Bill with coded details of cocaine prices. A small address book was also in the wallet.

We arranged to meet up with Vince Castle. He was a Gloucester Detective Sergeant and a key member of the Julie Squad. The meet was in a secluded spot. Eric handed him the wallet. Vince went off alone to copy the documents for evidential purposes. On his return with the original documents, he made a point of asking how we were. Vince was a great guy and a good detective. I sensed there was a hidden agenda. Asking him what lay behind the question, he told us that Lee was becoming worried about us.

We had now been deep undercover for six months and Lee was anxious about our welfare, as was Vince. We shrugged it off and reassured him that we were fine. Dick Lee, in his book[11] would have it that he was so concerned, he invited us to see him and Vince Castle at Bronwydd, the rented cottage that housed the Kemp/Bott surveillance team. That was incorrect. Or, as they say in Liverpool – a load of bollocks! Eric and I never went there and in fact, to this day, I have no idea about its location. Vince Castle returned the telegram and address book to us. In turn, we replaced them in Blue's wallet in exactly the same state as we had found them. The following day we returned the wallet and its contents to an unsuspecting Blue.

• • •

The telephone intercept was still intact at Y Glyn. One conversation excited Lee. It appeared Spenceley was arranging to meet Smiles for a handover of a large quantity of LSD. The handover was planned to take place in a pub called the Black Lion in Lampeter. Lee asked us to go to this pub and observe the handover, first enquiring if we felt it safe to do so. Our view was that the venue was a pub. It was nearby in Lampeter. It followed that we felt Smiles would not have become paranoid about seeing us in a pub in Lampeter. Pubs were our natural habitat. The layout of the pub was such that Smiles and Buzz did not see us. We could see them, but Spenceley failed to show up.

Lee asked us to cover that proposed handover because of what was heard on a phone tap. It is unusual for telephone intercepts to be openly discussed. At the outset of this book, I mentioned the Official Secrets Act. As a former police officer,

I am bound by its terms. Its purpose is to prevent disclosure of sensitive information. There are incidents of surveillance I mention in this book that are sensitive. There will be no attempt by me to provide you with any extra information. There will be nothing above and beyond that already in the public domain. I need to protect my own legal position. But my overwhelming motive is to protect certain individuals from identification. They know who they are. Their help was invaluable to the success of this massive investigation.

One subject that usually falls under the head of the Official Secrets Act is telephone intercepts. That's phone-tapping, to most people. During my time on Operation Julie we called it a facility. It is in the public domain and was so at an early stage following the conclusion of the investigation. It was public knowledge that the Operation Julie Squad utilised these intercepts. The intercepted telephone calls, recorded and then transcribed, were an invaluable tool. Smiles, or rather the telephone in his home, was the subject of a facility for some time. It was of great assistance to me on one occasion.

As a drugs squad detective in Hampshire, I had dealings with a young man from the Aldershot area. Aldershot is known as the home of the British Army. It has many regiments and other military facilities occupying a huge area just off the civilian town centre. The surrounding location is full of military career professionals, both ranking and non-ranking officers. One feature of army life is mobility.

That led to many kids from army family backgrounds being farmed out to boarding schools. That lifestyle was a catalyst for producing many wayward young men and women. They were from a privileged background but seemed determined to kick out against society. Many of them turned to drugs as a way of life. Robert was one of them.

Robert was a suspected local drug dealer in the Aldershot and Farnborough area of Hampshire. The intelligence on him and the informant's words were that he was selling drugs at a local college for 16–18-year-olds. LSD and cannabis were said to be his main stock-in-trade. A search warrant was obtained and I, along with one other drugs squad officer, carried out the search. Nothing much was found. Robert did leave me with an impression that has lasted to this day. He was one of the most obnoxious people I have ever met. He was a spoiled rich kid who just loved to irritate people in general, the more so if they happened to be "pigs!" Robert was about 23 years old and didn't work but drove around in a newish VW Beetle. The number of that Beetle was etched into my memory.

During our daily reporting procedure from a secluded public telephone, we were kept updated on anything of interest. That included anything from the facility on Smiles's telephone. Collie said this one day:

'Someone called Robert phoned and said he was on his way [to Smiles's home] to collect the goods. He said he would be leaving Aldershot later as he had to wait until the Volkswagen dealer had finished servicing his car. Mr Lee asks you to look out for this car and obtain details.'

On hearing this I thought, *Fuck! Shit! I know Robert! More to the point, he knows me!*

A chance encounter with Robert could have blown my cover. Not only that, but it would also jeopardise the whole Operation Julie investigation. The facility had proved invaluable but not for the reason it was first intended.

It enabled Eric and me to come up with a plan. We drove back to our cottage, passing Y Glyn on the way. There was a blue VW Beetle parked outside. I knew the car before I even looked at the number plate. Even though no one was in the car, I slid down in the passenger seat of the van to try and make myself invisible. I was not going to take the chance that the obnoxious Robert was going to exit Smiles's house just as we were passing by.

There was a time lag between the two calls – the making of the call by Robert to Smiles and the contents of that call notified to us. By the time the contents of the telephone tap reached our ears, Robert was already in situ. I can tell you it was tempting to bust this obnoxious young man there and then, complete with his bag of acid from Smiles. It was tempting to have him stopped on his way back to Hampshire and arrested with enough acid tabs to ensure the courts would find him a dealer. Then the court would imprison him for two or three years. Common sense ruled, as did the notion of the greater good. It was vital to let the distribution chain do its thing until the day we finally struck.

• • •

One of our regular drinking haunts was the Railway in Tregaron. We enjoyed an evening-long drinking session with Happy and Buzz in there one mid-December day. All four us went on to a dance in Tregaron Hall before we dropped off Buzz at Smiles's home in the early hours.

The dance had been a little boring for me. I went outside to the van, taking a few cans of beer with me. We had parked the van at the rear of the hall. I decided to open up the back doors and sit on the floor of the van, legs dangling out, and drink my beer. A young girl appeared from nowhere. She had long red hair down to her waist and looked about 15 years old. I was wary when she spoke to me in a friendly way.

'Hello,' she said in her best lilting Welsh accent. *Must be local. Pretty. Too young. Jailbait.*

'I'm April,' she said.

'Hi, I'm Steve.'

She sat down next to me, close and comfortable, placing her hand on my thigh.

'I saw you inside the hall. You looked bored.'

'Yep! Didn't know it showed.'

'I followed you out. I'm bored too.'

'How can you be bored? You must have all the boys chasing you.'

'That's the problem. They are all boys. The locals are stupid boys, too.'

'Hmm.'

'I like older men. They know what they are doing.'

'You are only fifteen.'

Her nostrils flared and she tossed back her hair.

Full of indignant righteousness, she said, 'I'm seventeen. Do you want to see my driving licence?'

She delved into her small clasp purse and pulled out a driving licence.

Holding it out, she said, 'Take a look.' It wasn't her licence. The photo was of an older woman.

She was jailbait. I decided to be harsh and said, 'Now, fuck off!'

April snarled back, 'You fuck off too, you prick!' She flounced off with an exaggerated swing of the hips to show me what I was missing.

I am no saint. I will stop looking at a pretty woman only when I am dead. But undercover or not, I knew where to draw a line.

• • •

This was a busy time in the run-up to Christmas. Socialising, drinking and smoking weed were all an integral part of a regular pattern. Smiles entertained us at his home on some more occasions. Sometimes he was joined by Mac, sometimes Buzz and on the infrequent occasion, Mary, Smiles's wife. If we weren't at Smiles's home or Blue's home, we were in a pub.

Smiles had long since quit the little Reagan and Carter joke he employed in the early days. He must have loved that show, *The Sweeney* (short form of Sweeney Todd – Cockney rhyming slang for the London Metropolitan Police Flying Squad). He loved referring to the characters played by John Thaw and Dennis Waterman. Often we heard the greeting by Smiles on walking into the pub. Affecting a John Thaw-like Manchester accent and aiming a 'Hello. It's Reagan and Carter,' in our direction.

On reflection, I am convinced he used to go into his little routine for two reasons. Smiles was a showman. He would stand out in a convention of extroverts. He only ever said it if there was an audience so he could bask in the humour of his making. Also, it was a sign in the early days that despite liking us, he was wary.

By December 1976, the wariness had gone. It was 16 December when Smiles approached me as I was taking a leak in the urinals at the back of the New Inn.

I was shaking off the residue when I heard Smiles say, 'Have a good Christmas.'

I turned around to see that familiar winter black-and-white check coat of his. Then the flashing white teeth before I saw his outstretched hand. He was grasping something in his clenched fist. As an automatic response, I held my open hand out. He placed the gift into my hand with an exhortation to 'Enjoy'. It was a small block of hash that glistened with freshness. If all else failed, he had now provided evidence of supplying a Class B drug.

A further factor in him resolving to quit *The Sweeney* routine was Eric's reaction one day. Smiles had only once challenged us full-on about whether we were cops. That was way back when we gave him a lift in the van from Lampeter to Llanddewi Brefi. Eric heard the Reagan and Carter routine one too many times. He decided on a different tactic. Eric did not touch him. Neither did he lay a hand on him, as some accounts would have it. He just verbally ripped into Smiles in front of all in the New Inn.

'If you come out with that fucking stupid joke one more time, I'll ram my fist down your throat, taking your precious fucking teeth as well!'

Eric had issued a similar warning to Smiles when Jan had accompanied him to Llanddewi Brefi.

On this occasion, Eric added – 'Don't talk to me about pigs. I fucking hate them. I'm still looking for my brother 'cause he got fitted up by the filth!'

The proverbial pin dropped and no one in the room heard it. It was an awkward silence and I was thinking, *Oh! Shit! That may have been a little over-acted!*

'Sorry, Eric. Nothing meant,' Smiles said.

We never heard the words Reagan, Carter or *The Sweeney* again.

We were in the New Inn until late on 23 December. Our cover story gave us an acceptable reason to return on 6 January 1977.

## TWENTY-ONE

# NEW YEAR

January 1977 started off slowly in Llanddewi Brefi. Possibly a hippie communal hangover? It was good to renew acquaintances in the New Inn once more. Smiles was on the usual good form and holding court in the New Inn. He was regaling me with stories about his Christmas at home. How he entertained a Dutch artist friend of his. Little did he know, we suspected that the Dutch artist friend was Tony Dalton, He was one of Smiles's two London dealers.

Travel to exotic places was always a subject for Smiles and one he enjoyed. He appeared to have a fascination with India. He opened up about other things. He told me that when working in London he was often tooled up – carrying a gun. He also added that he used to keep a gun upstairs at his home, Y Glyn. Shortly after the New Year, Smiles was absent from the village for a while. Mary, his wife, told me he would soon be back.

Before our return to Wales, we had a full day in the squad office at Devizes. The tension was running high. It was all too plain that the pressure on Lee to wrap up was intense. For my part, I was becoming angry at this pressure. It felt like a waste of time if the plug was pulled too early. We had not achieved our goals of taking out the whole manufacturing process, not to mention the higher echelons of the distribution network.

I had returned to Wales refreshed after a fashion after the break. But I was beginning to realise the work was taking its toll on my wellbeing. The excess drinking and smoking of cannabis were harming me both in body and mind. That, combined with the stresses of the role, resulted in side effects. I had become irritable and snappy. More to the point, I was keen to remain in my alter ego persona. I was more comfortable in the skin of Steve Jackson than that of Steve Bentley.

The Christmas period also allowed me to reflect on my private social life since working undercover. It no longer existed. I could not socialise for fear of being asked too many questions by friends, acquaintances and family. I saw my parents and sister once only during the whole time undercover. My mother appeared shocked by seeing my long hair and beard. I think she was even more shocked about seeing my dirty jeans – 'No, Mum. I don't want you to wash them.' She had difficulty understanding my new persona.

I had to be stern with my sister, who is six years younger than me. She showed too much curiosity. I could not be sure she wouldn't gob off to her friends. So I told her to keep her mouth shut unless she wanted to see me lying dead in a ditch one day. My sister still reminds me of that. I saw my brother twice during my time undercover. He is one person I would move heaven and earth for if it became necessary. (It's still difficult for me to use the past tense. He died suddenly in 2002.) Once, I saw him at Devizes when we had a curry together. The second time was a few weeks later in Bournemouth when I met a few of his fellow chef pals. Before I agreed to meet him and his pals, I sought a reassurance that they too would keep quiet about my new role. One of my brother's chef pals, Ricky Abbotts, is still a friend today. He continues to remind me of how I looked back then and how I refused to answer questions about what I was doing.

My cricketing and footballing activities had been suspended. I did not want colleagues and teammates asking questions. On the occasions I did spend at home, I stayed indoors. No wonder I felt more comfortable in the skin of Steve Jackson. He was a free bird. The real me was caged.

• • •

The telephone intercept at Y Glyn had gone. It was needed elsewhere. Particularly as the existence of 23 Seymour Road, Hampton Wick, Greater London, emerged. Henry Todd had bought a large suburban detached house using the false name of J. J. Ross. The conjecture was Seymour Road could be the new acid-manufacturing laboratory. Or could there be two existing side-by-side in Britain and supplying millions of LSD tabs?

It was in January 1977 that Lee notoriously pronounced, 'No way is there a lab in Seymour Road!' He was to be remorselessly teased about that remark in the future.

## TWENTY-ONE

It was now the fag end of January and yet again we joined Smiles and Happy for drinks in the New Inn. Smiles was even chattier than usual. He was talking about the fact he had been snowed in over the weekend, a clear reference to cocaine. He also spoke about tripping on acid over Christmas with his Dutch friend. We all were in favour of a change of scenery. I sensed a big drinking session was imminent. So we set off in the van for the Talbot in Tregaron. Smiles called Mary to let her know where he was going. He was considerate.

After a few rounds of drinks Smiles was the first to start chatting to a large heavily built black guy who went by the name of Zane. He was fun and possessed the most infectious belly laugh. He accepted Smiles's invitation to return to Y Glyn for more partying. Smiles hand-rolled what was now the obligatory joint. In fact, he did this twice on returning to his house.

What happened next took me by surprise a little. It was a sign that he trusted us one hundred per cent. Smiles produced a small, ebony-coloured figurine, about nine inches high. He unscrewed the top and produced a bag of white powder. Placing the bag on the table, he then placed another ebony-coloured item on the table. This time a shiny smooth flat board with several lines scored down the middle from end to end.

Smiles emptied some of the powder onto the flat board and, using a razor blade, chopped it. The powder looked fine in texture when it left the bag but soon became finer through chopping. He arranged it so it formed straight lines occupying the grooves in the middle of the board. Smiles's wallet seemed to be full of £20 notes. He pulled one out and rolled it up, then snorted a whole line of coke. It disappeared up his nostril in about one second flat. It was my turn next.

This was an escalation of the challenges facing me in my undercover role. *What to do? Do I make some kind of excuse? Run the risk that the excuse is seen as feeble?* Cocaine was and still is a Class A drug and is known for being addictive. All these thoughts clattered away inside my head.

I took hold of the rolled-up £20 note from Smiles and bent down over the board. There were four lines remaining. Without hesitation, I snorted one entire line through my nostril.

Smiles, throughout this cocaine ceremony, kept repeating the same mantra.

'This is not any old street shit. It's ninety per cent pure Colombian!' He did like to impress.

I have no idea to this day whether it was 90 per cent pure. I do know that it made me feel like flying! I could have walked through a brick wall, engaged a fierce enemy, wrestled a grizzly bear or gone five rounds with Muhammad Ali! It made me feel handsome, vital and dashing. It filled me with so much confidence that I wanted to bottle it and sell it. It felt that good. That memory of the cocaine buzz stayed with me for many, many years. The buzz lasted for some time that day undoubtedly helped by a second bump before Smiles, Mary, Zane and I went out to the Lampeter restaurant.

Smiles decided to treat us all to a meal. One problem – that would mean no babysitter. Eric volunteered and his offer was accepted with sincere gratitude by both Mary and Smiles. Smiles, Mary, Buzz, Zane and I travelled by taxi to the restaurant. On the way, I had a thought, *Cute Eric, very cute* – I hoped he was going to do what I would have done if we had reversed roles. He did and was bursting to tell me all about it the following morning.

The evening in the Lampeter restaurant was a hoot from start to finish, no doubt assisted by the cocaine. We all, except Eric, ingested a second line while waiting for the taxi at Y Glyn. We must have been a raucous bunch, even boorish. None of us cared. Smiles was in a particularly generous mood and picked up the tab for the whole evening.

We consumed several bottles of champagne and many obligatory shots of bourbon. My confidence, enhanced by coke, enabled me to chat with ease with all the women in the restaurant. Chat and flirt. I felt witty, even in my thoughts, comparing myself to Oscar Wilde or Winston Churchill. Those thoughts were instigated by Smiles's brand of witticisms. He was fond of saying, 'You will, Oscar, you will,' in reference to the Whistler/Wilde story about Wilde encountering James McNeill Whistler during high-society gathering.

That evening he also used the phrase, 'I would challenge you to a battle of wits, but I see you are unarmed.' Smiles was wrong in his attribution of that to Churchill. My flirting also extended to Mary. Smiles did not object. She was devoted to Smiles. I knew that when flirting with her but carried on. Her beautiful rounded smiling face and blue eyes attracted me from day one. She had beautiful natural blonde hair and gentle nature. In any event, I had the feeling that she liked me flirting with her.

Still in high spirits, we grabbed a taxi to return to Y Glyn. About twenty minutes later we entered Smiles' home to find Eric watching TV and sprawled out on the sofa. He was so casual he didn't even speak as we poured into the room. A raised hand was his signal of acknowledgement that there was some new activity in the house. Mister Cool! We took our leave and I slept like a log back at the cottage.

It strikes me as I look back on the Llanddewi Brefi Log some forty years later (where did the time go?) that we became far more explicit in reporting our drug-taking as time went by. Initially, we kind of hinted at it but then we logged specifics about the chillum events and the snorting of coke. Why was this?

First, we were past caring. Here is an example that we were at first careful about what we logged. Okay, it's in a non-drugs context. It was the entry surrounding Doug and the smashed window in Tregaron. There was no mention that it was me who had pushed him through the shop window. Second, we were suffering from battle fatigue. It was our unsubtle coded signal to get us the hell out of there.

Third, it was clear the end was in sight. The activity and excitement mounted in relation to Seymour Road. No one seemed to give a shit about us stuck in the middle of Wales!

The morning after the night in the Lampeter restaurant, Eric told his tale. He recounted the covert search story to me. He grinned all the way through telling it.

Eric left the best bit to last. He went into detail about how he had carried out the covert search of Smiles's home. He took full advantage while we were all cavorting on cocaine at the Lampeter restaurant. He noted that there were no bolts on the back door. There was only a mortice lock. He was thinking ahead to the time when that door would be broken down – at the same time as countless other doors throughout Britain on the day of reckoning. Eric described how he was careful to leave no trace of his activities.

Eric went into some detail, but I knew he was holding back. He covered stuff such as checking for hidden compartments. He said there was an apparent removal of a fireplace in one room. He thought there was a likely hiding place for the chillum in the kitchen just above where the stovepipe entered the ceiling space. His tale lingered in the kitchen and he could not contain himself any longer.

'Guess what else I found?'

'Dick Lee's acid lab?'

'Oh! Fuck off! Do you want to know or what?'

'You're going to tell me anyway, so tell.'

'A plastic bag stuffed full of cash. That's not all. There

was a cereal packet with, I guess, at least a thousand acid tabs in it.'

Eric found this stash in cereal boxes underneath the kitchen worktop. We later learned that hiding the acid tabs in cereal packets was a common tactic used by the Julie distributors.

. . .

Later that day Happy came to our cottage. He had a message for us from Smiles. We had been summoned to the New Inn for yet another bout of heavy drinking. We obliged. The company in the pub comprised of Zane, who had stayed the night at Smiles's home; Buzz, Happy, Smiles, of course; Eric and me. Buzz was starting to become complacent, as was Smiles.

During this session Buzz spoke to Smiles, asking him if Mon was working. They were talking in code but we knew who Mon was. She was Monica Kenyon, later arrested and convicted as a part of the Operation Julie conspiracy. She was the partner of Tony Dalton, one of Smiles's London connections. Following this session, Smiles went shopping in Lampeter for a wedding present for Happy. It was a generous, expensive present and so typical of Smiles.

## TWENTY-TWO

# COP KILLER

February 1977 saw the leaving of Llanddewi Brefi for Steve Jackson and Eric Walker. They never returned and neither did Steve Bentley or Eric Wright.

Lee was not only anxious about the current location of the acid lab or labs, but also the political pressures. He was also anxious about us. He must have been aware of our explicit entries in the Llanddewi Brefi Log. In particular, the use of drugs by his men. We had served our purpose. The cocaine importation plot involving Blue and Bill was supposedly now the remit of the DEA to deal with in America. The telephone intercept on Y Glyn had ceased and it was time for Lee to pull us out. He told us to start preparing another cover story to explain our prolonged absence from the village. Before we left, Eric and I had a fright.

We had covered some miles in the van, our trusty friend. There had never been any collisions or road traffic accidents. Until now. I was driving the van in a narrow stretch of a country lane just outside of Tregaron. I slowed down as another car headed toward me. The other driver tried to speed past me and clipped the front of our van. I stopped and so did the driver of the other car. Before I got out, I winked at Eric because I felt like a bit of play-acting.

Eric told me that I scared the shit out of the other driver who admitted it was his fault. Now we have the dilemma of exchanging details as required by the law. I say dilemma, even though we had fake driving licences and the van had a ghost plate. It was a dilemma in that it was an unnecessary hassle. A POLAC (Police Accident Report) was a lengthy document. That was bad enough. But it was not designed for circumstances like this. In any case, we couldn't tell him we were cops. Eric thought on his feet. He had a snout (informant or CI) in Bristol he trusted. He gave the snout's address. This was so the insurance company had a contact address.

This caused panic back in the office at Devizes. The squad office arranged for a mail intercept on the informant's flat, ensuring the retrieval of the insurance company letters. Rather than complicate matters, the other driver received a pleasant surprise. He received a cheque in the mail. I guess that is a first. A driver got an unexpected and undeserved insurance pay-out. After he admitted liability! It was less complicated for the police insurance company to pay up.

• • •

There was one more incident of note to take place in Llanddewi Brefi or, to be more accurate, Tregaron before we bid our farewell.

Our relationship with Smiles was now perfect from our point of view. It was another day in the New Inn like many others before. It started out with a few friendly drinks and friendly banter. That was before someone suggested a change of scenery. That usually spelt out a heavy drinking session. This day was no different. Eric, Smiles and I arrived at the Railway Steps pub in Tregaron. We met Happy and Buzz. Smiles was now frank and open in his conversations. Once more he claimed to have supplied Joan Armatrading with drugs back in his Birmingham days. He added that it was when she lived in Balsall Heath. He went into detail about tripping on acid, saying that the local mountains were his favoured location for dropping an acid tab.

The Blue episode involving us and cocaine must have been playing on the mind of Smiles. In a most direct way, he asked that we let him know if we had access to any quantities of cocaine, saying he would buy it from us. Smiles added that he was expecting a guy named Tony to bring him a pound weight of coke, but he could not rely on that.

This was as clear a sign as possible that Smiles now trusted us. He believed we were connected enough for him to score cocaine from us. We believed that by the reference to Tony he was talking about Tony Dalton. What we were not aware of at that time was information to which only Dick Lee was privy. One of Lee's faults was a tendency to keep certain things close to his chest.

I later became aware of the significance of this request from Smiles. UK Customs had briefed Dick Lee that they were about to raid Smiles's home in connection with a plot to import large amounts of cocaine. A Customs surveillance had seen Smiles and Tony Dalton when they visited an American, Frank Manacheo. This was at an address in Elgin Crescent, London.

The visit took place just before Christmas in 1976, shortly before the time of this conversation. The American was a wanted fugitive in the States. He was indicted there for a massive cocaine shipment the DEA had seized in New York. UK Customs believed Smiles and Dalton were planning a deal with Manacheo. They were going to exchange a large quantity of LSD for Manacheo's cocaine. Lee never made Eric and me aware of that development. It was a gross oversight on his part and may have had disastrous consequences for both of us. In my opinion, Americans, large cocaine shipments and gun violence are constant companions. Furthermore, what if there had been a connection between Manacheo, Bill and Blue? I admired Dick Lee for his risk-taking approach but not when it endangered my wellbeing!

The drinking started at about noon in the New Inn. It continued in the Railway Steps for the rest of the day. The pattern involved drinking three or four pints of beer followed by rounds of bourbon, Scotch whisky or Irish whiskey, then vodka. It was then back to a few rounds of beer again and the pattern repeated. We were all rat-assed!

It was gone official closing time in the pub. It was late at night. Apart from our inebriated posse, there were a handful of drinkers left. There were a few in the bar and the landlord and two staff. The staff were cleaning off tables and collecting empty glasses from abandoned tables. We had an array of unconsumed beverages on our table. No one came near us to clear it away as they knew we had every intention of drinking it all before we left the pub.

PC Lake was a local police officer and we had heard that he was a little too friendly with Smiles. Lake had no idea who Eric and I were.

The unmistakable uniformed figure of PC Lake loomed large in the front door of the pub. It wasn't so much what he said, it was the way he said it. It raised my hackles.

'You lot. Out!' boomed PC Lake's command.

'Fuck off!' I boomed back.

'Be gone by the time I come back,' he added before turning on his heels and walking off into the damp, dark night.

A silence followed Lake's rude interruption and my response. Gales of laughter broke the silence. Smiles, Happy and Buzz were loving it.

There were still several drinks on our table some twenty minutes later. The air was once more penetrated with the same booming police command.

'I told you lot to be gone,' Lake now had his truncheon drawn and hammered it on the serving bar top twice in succession. *Thump! Thump!* He stood there tapping the business end of the truncheon into the palm of his empty hand.

'And I told you to fuck off!' I responded. Lake was provoking me by his unnecessary demeanour.

Lake's jaw dropped for a moment. I guess no one had ever spoken to him in that manner during the whole of his police service.

I sensed hesitation on his part.

I was so far gone in drink and in my role, I did not consider backing down. If anything, I wanted it to escalate. I tried my best to do that.

'Come near me or my drink and I will ram that fucking stick up your shitty arse.'

Lake spluttered, 'What did you say?'

'Fuck off out of my sight now or I'll fucking kill you. You cunt!'

Lake left, much to my initial surprise. Within a few moments, it dawned on me why he did leave following my threat. I meant it. I was so in the moment of living the lie. I also knew that I had a literal get out of jail card. I was willing to risk an arrest for assault on Lake. I could use the ploy of contacting the senior officer without destroying our cover. I doubt that card would have exonerated me from all the consequences if I had seriously injured him.

Smiles and Eric took hold of my arms.

'Look, we've had fun but we need to go,' Smiles counselled.

Drunk as I was, I recognised the wisdom of those words. It also gave me an honourable retreat without losing face.

As we left the pub, Lake was stood about 20 yards away. Once more, he was tapping his truncheon in the palm of his hand. I gained the impression that this business wasn't over yet.

PC Lake started to walk toward us. Happy was the first to run. Like lemmings approaching the cliff, we followed suit.

Fortunately, Lake's athleticism had long gone. It had probably disappeared with his youth. Following Happy, we made it to the sanctuary of his home. We stayed motionless for some time in the darkness of the house. Satisfied Lake had not followed us, we all roared with laughter.

Smiles turned to me, grinning: 'Cop killer!'

I later heard that became my name in Llanddewi Brefi. We were now assimilated in full into the environment, even if we had not been before.

No sooner had that night passed it was time to go. Lee and London were calling; Hendon and 23 Seymour Road were the next stops on the journey.

Say goodbye to Steve Jackson! I wish it had been that easy.

## TWENTY-THREE

# NO WAY A LAB AT SEYMOUR ROAD

Seymour Road and Hendon was a perfect way to recuperate. Both Eric and I joined up with the surveillance teams based in Hendon.

The teams were living their off-duty hours in a 4-bedroom detached house near RAF Hendon in north London. It was a house usually used by an RAF officer and his family. This was another example of Dick Lee's wheeling and dealing. The accommodation was a must to house the London surveillance teams. Housing the teams in police accommodation were not viable. We had to keep secrets from the Metropolitan Police. The RAF house was a perfect answer to the problem.

As the crow flies, the accommodation was not too far from Seymour Road in Hampton Wick. But the drive was a tedious journey along the west part of London's North Circular Road then the A3 until the exit at Kingston-Upon-Thames or across Kew Bridge through Richmond. It was to become a regular trip from February through March 1977. Although there were four bedrooms, many of us occupied the house. We split into two shifts to provide 24-hour surveillance so that eased the problem of finding a bed.

## TWENTY-THREE

The sense that the end was nigh was prevalent among the team. Most of us now believed that 23 Seymour Road was a lab for the manufacturing and tabletting of the LSD. Todd, Cuthbertson and Munro, the chemist (these three were manufacturing, tabletting and distributing the LSD in and from London as opposed to Kemp's Welsh manufacturing facility at Carno), were often observed at Seymour Road. Surveillance was undertaken both by means of following in cars and, in the case of Munro, on foot. We were adept, efficient and professional in our surveillance techniques, aided by some high-tech kit.

Let me just say that we had 23 Seymour Road and the conspirators under constant scrutiny. Nothing escaped our gaze. As the weeks went by, the pressure on Lee to strike was enormous. He was waiting for one final piece of evidence before making the decision to move in on the gang. One vital piece of evidence to trigger the final denouement.

The breakthrough came as a result of one of the endless follows of Todd's Volvo. On leaving Seymour Road, Todd took a direct route to Reading in Berkshire. We followed him all the way to his final destination. Over Kew Bridge, onto the elevated section of the M4 Motorway and then again when he took the exit for the A33 into Reading. Shortly after that he made a sudden turn off toward the municipal dump, a site used to tip unwanted garbage.

We often bemoaned the cars donated to us by the eleven police forces for surveillance. They were all clapped out with too many miles on the clock. They were also in the main standard 1100 cc engines, such as the Hillman Avenger that I often drove. Yet they were also a blessing. That type of car was so commonplace that it didn't attract attention. They were boring, small family saloons. If Todd was wary of surveillance, the sight of a standard Hillman Avenger in his rear-view mirror was a good thing. It would not have warranted a second glance. There is more to surveillance than just following a vehicle. I decline to elaborate as it is sensitive information.

It wasn't possible to keep eyes on Todd and the Volvo all the way into the site without discovery. We watched from a safe distance. He grabbed items from the back of the Volvo and threw them among the myriad items of household waste. Todd talked to a guy in a Hi-Vis vest, assumed to be an employee at the site.

The Volvo left the site and went back to Seymour Road, followed there by most of the team. Alan Buxton was on our team that day. Known as Bucky, he was a Birmingham Regional Crime Squad detective, seconded to the Operation Julie Squad. We stayed behind at the site. Our eyes were glued on the items jettisoned by Todd. As we got closer, we could see the guy in the high-vis vest shovelling waste over the suspect items. He was driving a small JCB with a loading shovel at the front using the shovel to lift up waste and drop it on Todd's waste.

'Stop!' We both shouted at once.

## TWENTY-THREE

The JCB driver appeared not to hear us over the noise of his diesel engine.

'Stop! Police!'

It felt strange for me to once more announce myself as police. It felt stranger still fishing in my Levi pockets for my identification warrant card.

He heard us and ceased shovelling, turning the engine off.

We showed our identification.

'I need you to uncover that stuff the Volvo just dropped off.'

'Oh, matey boy (Todd) just gave me two quid to bury it, so what the fuck am I supposed to do now?'

'I'll tell you exactly what the fuck you are supposed to do now. Here's a fiver, now fucking uncover it! After that, you will make a statement about it all. Right?'

'Okey-dokey.'

Those items were the final pieces of evidence for which we were all waiting. They were rushed to Nigel Dunnett at the Home Office lab and he later confirmed what we were hoping.

Lee was ecstatic and we weren't far behind him. Plans were now laid to execute the arrests and raids on the main conspirators including the manufacturers, the distributors, dealers and their homes throughout Britain and overseas.

On our return to Hendon from Reading, we felt both hopeful and confident that the action at the Reading tip was to prove fruitful. We had to wait until the following day for Dunnett to make confirmation. On the way back to Hendon, Alan Buxton was pumped up. The weather had turned nasty with a strong wind and driving rain. It was the sort of conditions that are not ideal for motorcycling.

We overtook many heavy trucks trundling along in the slow lane on the motorway. One of them had a limpet attached to it! To shelter from the driving rain and wind, Bucky was grinning at us, holding onto the back of a truck with one hand on the truck while steering the motorbike with the other! The stuff of legend! Bucky was a hell of a character and loved telling us the tale of how he played the drums for Roy Orbison in the Big O's early British tours.

The time between the Reading tip find and the arrests and raids were a blur. Lee had brought in extra people and expertise to plan and execute the denouement. It was to be professionally run like a major inquiry such as a murder or other serious crime. This called for specialists.

One of the most notable specialists was Detective Superintendent Harry Atkinson, a man who had extensive experience of major crime inquiries. He made the office really tick both before and after the busts.

The planning of the arrests was detailed, with nothing left to chance. The decision was made to bring forward in time the execution of the search warrant at 23 Seymour Road because Todd had cancelled the milk delivery, sparking the justified notion that Todd and the others in the house were going on holiday. They were, as they had finished the acid production run. Both Eric and I were in this group, which was to gain entry to Todd's house. It was just reward. We were to arrest the occupants and search for evidence.

## TWENTY-THREE

### The Bust

Lensbury is a social venue alongside the banks of the River Thames at Teddington. It comprises of acres of sports playing fields and a clubhouse. It was the scene of our briefing on Friday, 25 March 1977 before we made our way to Seymour Road. The briefing in a small room in the pavilion was abuzz with excitement. We had been working toward this moment for a long time.

Dick Lee led the briefing and we listened with care to every word. The raiding group consisted of Detective Sergeants Johnny McWalter (Mac), Keith Campbell, Alan Morgan, and Ray Shipway. The Detective Constables included Alan Buxton (Bucky), Alan Jeffrey and, of course, Eric and me. There was also a small group of Scenes of Crime Officers (SOCOs) who were going to search the house and gather evidence. This group included Roger Corney from Hampshire, DC Keith Savory and Wiltshire's Wally Dodge. All three later experienced an unwanted acid trip. They ingested LSD as they searched the detached house at 23 Seymour Road. It happened while they were rolling up an old carpet. Munro had soaked the carpet with spilt acid during the manufacturing process.

At exactly 2005 hours (8.05 pm – "2005 hours" used as the briefings/searches/arrests were planned with a military-like precision) that day we entered 23 Seymour Road with a crash and a bang and a loud yell of 'Geronimo!'

The raiding party had split up. Some went to the front while others went to the rear of the house that was in darkness. I was in the detachment that clambered over a fence at the rear. As we approached the rear French windows, I turned to grin at Eric who was alongside me.

I saw his lips move and heard him shout 'Geronimo!'

At the same time, one of our group had swung a large bar, breaking the glass windows. For some strange reason, Eric, to this day, denies he had uttered this war cry. Maybe he was so pumped up he subconsciously let it all out?

Adrenaline abounded! We shattered the peace and boredom of London's suburbia. The suburban good life depicted in the TV show based on nearby Surbiton was about to cease for some. The air filled with the sounds of crashing glass. Glass splintered into many shards.

Police officers shouted, 'Police, stay still. Don't move!' I heard movement. I could hear people running, footsteps like giant scurrying mice. It was mayhem for a while. It felt a little scary. We did not know what we would find. Would there be violence?

The noise abated and I could make out the soothing sound of classical music coming from a room in the house. I made my way to the front living room by way of the hall. Todd loomed large in the hall. He looked menacing and defiant. I sensed he had a fight in him. But two officers had restrained Todd. There was no need for my help. I saw Munro, the LSD chemist, and Brian Cuthbertson in the front room. There was also a woman present. DC Jeffrey and I approached Cuthbertson. He was our target. That was part of our brief. We identified ourselves.

DC Jeffrey arrested him and told him we had a search warrant.

Cuthbertson said, 'There's a lot of you.'

If only he knew then what was to follow. Over 800 police officers nationwide would be conducting dawn raids the following morning. Perhaps then he would have revised his observation that there were a lot of us. We found a small quantity of hash and coke with Cuthbertson and he denied they belonged to him.

Eric and I saddled up together as partners in policing for one more time. We drove Cuthbertson to Swindon Police Station. We arrived at 10.15pm. He was put through the normal booking-in procedure and locked in a cell. *Clang!* The heavy iron door slammed shut.

At Swindon Police Station, a passing uniformed police officer stopped me. He pointed out that I was leaving a trail of blood behind me. Sure enough, there was blood oozing from a cut on my right little finger. It came back to me that I had grabbed hold of the French window frame at Seymour Road just after the glass was smashed. Immediately, I had felt slight pain but had pushed it to the back of my mind in the rush of adrenaline. Eric and I went to the Princess Margaret Hospital, Swindon, where I had some stitches inserted. A pretty nurse was inquisitive about what we had been doing.

We couldn't tell her a thing except to tell her to read the papers over the next few days.

It was going to be a long night. Briefings were to take place all over England, Wales and Scotland. They were to co-ordinate the raids on anyone connected to the Operation Julie investigation. Todd, Cuthbertson and Munro were all in custody at Swindon Police Station. None of them could make the usual phone call from the police station in case they tried to alert others. On leaving the hospital at Swindon, we had two choices: get some hard-earned sleep or make our way down the M4 to Tintagel House, London. Still high on adrenaline, we opted for the latter.

In 1977, Tintagel House was a 12-floor concrete and glass government building. It sat along the River Thames at Lambeth. It housed some departments of the Metropolitan Police Service (MPS). It also had a reputation of hosting secretive departments of the MPS. The fifth floor of the building was used to hold a briefing for the London-wide Operation Julie raids. The Flying Squad was excluded from the Tintagel House briefing. The same was true for other CID departments. There could be no risk of leaks.

The Special Patrol Group (SPG) was there in force. Elite uniformed officers of the SPG, a forerunner of the Territorial Support Group. The group had a fearsome reputation that later become notorious. It was a strange feeling to have them look at Eric and me with respect in their eyes. They were real police.

We were just observers at this briefing. The memory of hardened Met SPG officers nodding to me as a mark of respect as they filed out after the briefing is one I will not forget. It was starting to dawn on me that we really had achieved something worthwhile. This realisation was not the only thing dawning. Daybreak was fast approaching, and I drove us back to Swindon for a deserved and overdue sleep. It was a drive that almost ended in disaster. I became so sleepy at the wheel on the M4 I fell asleep while doing more than 70mph! The rumble strips between lanes woke me up with their signature staccato beat. I lived to tell this tale.

# TWENTY-FOUR

# OLD ACQUAINTANCES

Our temporary accommodation was a single-man's hostel annexe of Swindon Police Station. It reminded me of the hostel adjoining Kirkby Police Station. Eric and I had separate but adjoining rooms. I awoke on Saturday, 26 March 1977, in my barrack-like room. Pulling back the curtain, I blinked at the sunlight outside the window. My eyes slowly adjusted. I have a regular wake-up routine of yawning and scratching various body parts, like most men, I think. While going through this routine, I saw a bleak view outside.

Swindon is full of concrete slab buildings. There was a Ford dealership at the back of the hostel room. It was no different to many other dreary concrete Swindon edifices. Then I did a double-take. I could not believe what I saw.

'Eric, Eric, Eric!' I yelled, hammering on his room door.

'What?' He opened the door to see me with the grin of a six-year-old schoolboy.

I flung open the curtains in his room, 'Look!'

'Well, fuck me!' was all Eric could say. Come to think of it, we both said a lot of 'fucks' in our time together, just like McNulty and Bunk in the hilarious but could-be-true murder re-enactment scene from HBO's *The Wire*[12].

The cause of this 'fuck me' was outside our windows. There was the large Ford sign on the wall of the dreary building with Walker and Jackson, the dealership name, under the distinctive blue and white Ford logo! Eric Walker and Steve Jackson!

That weekend was interview time. Dick Lee had drawn up a list of all the conspirators including those responsible for manufacturing and tabletting LSD both past and present, in Wales and Hampton Wick. Then came the list of the main distribution network: Cuthbertson, Fielding, Spenceley, Smiles. Two detectives were assigned to each suspected conspirator. They were responsible for conducting interviews. Martyn Pritchard and I were allocated Nigel 'Leaf' Fielding.

Lee has maintained he chose his interviewing partners with care. Maybe he did. Did he give any thought to the pairing of Martyn and me? If so, it must have been along these lines: Martyn was a talented undercover officer. He could talk the hind leg off a donkey and spoke like a head. He was disorganised and thus there was no structure to his interviewing technique. I was the polar opposite.

So, it followed that Pritchard did most of the talking during the interviews with Fielding.

Most of the Saturday was spent in preparing interview notes to talk to Fielding. Martyn was now a Detective Sergeant. He had been recently promoted. We started the interview shortly after lunch on Sunday, 27 March. At first,

Fielding insisted on his right to have a solicitor present. It soon became clear he was reluctant to involve his wife. At that point, Martyn seemed to be developing a rapport with our interviewee, so I left the room to organise some tea and refreshments.

On my return with the tea, Fielding was in full flow. He explained that he got microdots from Cuthbertson and Todd (but he knew Todd only as George). He told us how he transported them to Russ Spenceley. Spenceley would pay £165 for a thousand. Fielding would receive £5 per thousand for acting as the courier.

He also started to explain his system of drop points – a system where he would hide the stash in a secluded forest later to be collected by someone else in the distribution chain. This is a system familiar to terrorist cells. Perhaps it was a nod to the influence of the shadowy figure of Ronald Stark?

Fielding was typical of many suspects. While he remained in custody, it must have been clear to him just how much we already knew. But, like others before him and many since he decided to drip-feed a succession of admissions to us. There wasn't much he could tell us about his history of dealing in acid. But we didn't know everything or every location of his stashes. Finally, he told us about a stash in the woods at Hartley Wintney in Hampshire.

Martyn Pritchard, Eric Wright, Alan Buxton and I drove to Hartley Wintney that night. We followed the directions Fielding had given us. Buried in a hole in the ground we found his stash of 100,000 acid tabs. That stood as a world record for a police drugs seizure by street value worldwide. At least it did for a few days. Then other Operation Julie officers unearthed even larger quantities.

On Tuesday, 29 March 1977, Fielding showed me exactly where his remaining stashes were. First, we went to Nine Mile Ride, near Wokingham, where he indicated two stash points in the woods. They were on Forestry Commission land and they were about 300 yards distant from each other. Both were now holes in the ground, about four feet deep. The first was empty. The other contained a large black plastic refuse bag with eight empty plastic containers.

I asked him to clarify the purpose of two holes. One was for the pick-up, he explained. He was supposed to watch the pick-up to prevent rip-offs but fell into the habit of not bothering as he felt paranoid standing about in the woods. The second hole with the containers was for storing the tabs he took from Brian Cuthbertson.

The interviewing of Fielding continued long into that same Tuesday. He admitted that he was dealing in quantities of 50–75,000 tabs at a time and had also handled 100,000 in one transaction – the tabs we had seized at Hartley Wintney. He mainly dealt with Cuthbertson. He had also dealt with George (Henry Todd) directly. Fielding volunteered that the Todd/Cuthbertson tabs came in two different forms – domes and dots – to dupe the police into thinking there were two separate sources.

## Smiles and I Meet in the Cell

The time soon came for renewing old acquaintances. Smiles was under arrest and occupying a cell at Swindon Police Station. I felt a need to see him but first cleared it with Dick Lee. I was apprehensive. I had no idea how Smiles would react but it was something I had to do.

I had the uniformed gaoler unlock the cell door. As it swung open, I saw the familiar face and hair of Smiles as he sat on the cell bench. He looked up slowly at me, not immediately seeming to recognise me. This could have been as a result of two things. First, he hadn't seen me since the night of the "cop killer" incident some two months earlier. Since that time, I had smartened up in my appearance a little and my hair was shorter though still long. My beard had gone and only a thick droopy moustache remained as facial hair. Second, after recognition kicked in, he was disoriented for a moment. I saw a flicker of incomprehension. He could not understand why a "cop killer" and cocaine dealer was about to share his cell with him. Then the penny dropped! The famous smile spread from east to west.

'No hard feelings, man. It's all part of the game,' is all Smiles said.

We hugged each other. Patted one another's back like long-lost buddies as if reacquainted for the first time in many years. I experienced a lump in my throat and a glistening around the eyes. There was a warm feeling that welled up in my chest as if I was embracing my own brother. Damn it! He could have been a brother!

It was a case of mutual respect from two men who were not that dissimilar in their outlooks on life. With an awkward clearing of my throat, I disengaged. I shook his right hand while holding on to his right forearm with my left hand. I hoped that he could not see my misty eyes as I made a conscious effort to avert his gaze. There was another reason for shying away from Smiles's gaze – I felt guilty about my deception. That feeling of guilt was to stay with me for a long time. It was nothing to do with the eight-year sentence of imprisonment passed on him.

I heard the solid metal cell door slam behind me as I walked away from Smiles's cell. I heard my footsteps echo down those soulless corridors. Man! I felt like crap. There was no sense of victory or jubilation. This was not a personal triumph. I hurried to my car, fumbled with the key in the ignition and flooded the engine with petrol. The damn old Cortina refused to start, and I slammed my fist down on the horn.

The blare of the horn was followed by a tap on the driver's window.

'Are you alright,' asked a fresh-faced uniformed copper.

'As a matter of fact, no, I'm not. Now be a good boy and fuck off. Leave me alone!'

Police Constable Freshface turned on his heels and walked away. Turning on the car radio, I heard 'Bohemian

Rhapsody.' It felt like I had pulled a trigger and shot a man, now he was dead. My chest heaved. I wiped away a tear. This was no victory. This was no war.

**Doug Again**

Eric and I met with Douglas John Flanagan again on 1 April at Devizes Police Station. He was unable to appreciate the April Fool's Day joke. Swindon Police Station was full, so after Doug's arrest he was taken to the police station in Devizes. We saw him in an interview room and he had no clue about who we were apart from two detectives. Asked why he thought he was in custody, he told us that a small amount of drugs was found on him. Correcting him, we informed him we were part of the Operation Julie investigation and we believed he was a part of the distribution network.

'You mean the acid thing? I heard about it from the papers. It sounds a bit heavy,' he said.

Every newspaper throughout Britain had published many column inches about the success of Operation Julie. That was partly due to several of the squad members making phone calls to every news desk in the country. Doug had been arrested a few days after the main busts. (Those synchronised raids involving 800 officers.) He was confirming that Operation Julie was the news item of the week!

We interviewed Doug several times. In the first interview, we told him about the day he was arrested in Tregaron for smashing the shop window. We even told him in which pub he had been drinking and that he had been talking to two guys about cutting trees down.

'Yeah, you're right. It was two guys with a power saw,' he said. Still no recognition!

On Monday, 4 April Doug consulted with a solicitor at court following his remand in custody. Of course, I have no idea what the solicitor said to him. But considering the previous court appearances of the main conspirators and distributors, the lawyer must have been aware of the mass of evidence. A huge amount of evidence accumulated by the Julie team. Whatever passed between that lawyer and his client, and it's not difficult to guess what the advice was. Doug decided to give Eric and me a fuller account of his involvement.

Doug went on to confirm that he was scoring his acid from Smiles and distributing it at street level in London. A deal of 10,000 tabs was commonplace and Doug assured us he was only making a profit of £7 per thousand. I came to doubt the accuracy of that statement. Moments later, Doug was asked about £306 found on him when arrested. He admitted it was drug money and he intended to post it to Smiles. None of it made sense, but it didn't matter. Doug had admitted enough to warrant his eventual conviction in the conspiracy. He was later sentenced to two years' imprisonment. The judge was accurate as he labelled him the 'last link in the chain' of the conspiracy. Jail sentences were also passed on two other lower-level dealers that Smiles supplied. Dealers who came to our notice during our time undercover in Llanddewi Brefi.

Doug's memory also returned, and he told us that he now remembered talking to us in Tregaron. He had no recollection of how he had come to fall through the shop window. We did not enlighten him. According to Doug, a tab of acid was selling on the street for £1.25 before the Julie busts and he had been dealing through Smiles for just over one year. He added that in the days following the Julie raids, one acid tab now cost £5 on the street.

Doug had one more thing to say before our final interview had concluded:

'You need to carry on now and crack down on the serious heroin and cocaine dealers. You know, the guys who never get their hands dirty, never see the product. There will be mayhem on our streets if nothing is done.'

Wise words from a low-level dealer in acid.

The interviews with Doug and Fielding brought up another point of interest. Both said they were acid dealers for the money. No highfalutin' idealistic stuff from them!

## TWENTY-FIVE

# RECALL PAPERS

Swindon was now our new HQ, not Devizes. It had been so from the day of entering 23 Seymour Road armed with a Misuse of Drugs Act search warrant until the end of the interviews. All the squad were based there. By all, I mean the Operation Julie Squad –the original 25 hand-picked detectives involved in the interviewing process.

We worked hard and played hard. Swindon Police Station had a social club bar. It must have seen its takings increase one hundredfold! There was a party atmosphere every night. The Brummie (natives of Birmingham) lads, particularly Bucky, were usually at the forefront of it. They managed to grab three white smock coats and stethoscopes from somewhere. They made a grand entrance into the social club looking like the Marx Brothers dressed as hospital doctors! It was hilarious as they agitated around the room in best Marx Brothers style.

The best came last. Posing as three psychiatrists, they bundled off Dick Lee laid out patient-like on top of a catering trolley! The *coup de grâce* was the exit of doctors and patient to the roar of, 'No way is there a lab in Seymour Road!'

That same night I took a phone call on the public telephone set in the small passage between the bar and the urinals. Martyn Pritchard had alerted me to it, telling me I had a woman on the phone wanting to speak to me. My curiosity sated when I heard Mary, Smiles's wife, and her seductive whispers. She was a little too obvious in her manner and it was clear Mary thought she was doing the right thing by her man. I thought she planned to compromise me in some way. It was a hare-brained plan anyway. The case against Smiles was overwhelming and did not rely on my evidence as a witness. For once, I thought with my brain and not my thing in my underpants. I told her I was sorry but there was nothing I could do. That was the truth.

The partying carried on whether we were in Swindon, Devizes, Bristol or Basingstoke. Basingstoke was still my home even after my promotion to Detective Sergeant. I was commuting from there to Devizes and Swindon on a regular basis until the loose ends were all tied up and the squad sadly had to be wound up. Pressure existed to establish a National Drugs Squad with Julie members at its core. Many of the advocates for it belonged to the media. The internal police decision-makers were having none of it. There was, as always, an infuriating intransigence towards fresh ideas and a solid resistance to any suspicion of elitism. Any thoughts of a national police agency were dismissed out of hand.

Doug, had he heard about the folly of this stance, would have been disappointed. After all, he was right. Heroin and cocaine addiction are now a huge problem. Crack cocaine appeared since Operation Julie; these drugs now account for most street crimes. Most crimes of burglary and robbery feed a habit.

Some of the final pieces of the Operation Julie jigsaw were to do with assets of the conspirators. Once more, Dick Lee was quick to spot the missing expertise. The squad inducted Detective Superintendent Gerry Squires. He came from the City of London Police Fraud Squad (experts in serious financial fraud and tracing assets) to spearhead the efforts in tracing assets and bank accounts, particularly those held in Swiss banks. But the time came when those enquiries were complete and the curtain finally fell. The show's over folks!

Yet, it wasn't quite over. The showpiece sentencing hearing, conducted by Mr Justice Park, took place the following year.

Finally, I received my recall papers to return to my force, the Hampshire Constabulary. Before my recall, I had a long chat with DI Peter Long, but this time it was nothing to do with expenses. Peter had the ear of Cyril 'Tanky' Holdaway, the man in charge of CID in Hampshire. Someone decided that my first posting back in my home force was CID at Tadley. They thought they were doing me a favour. Nothing could be further from the truth.

Tadley in 1977/78 was a small town. Its main purpose was to provide housing for the workers at the Atomic Weapons Research Establishment (AWRE) in nearby Aldermaston, Berkshire. The police station was also small, housing the entire Tadley force of one uniformed Sergeant and four uniformed constables. Then there was me. I was the Tadley CID!

Anything that sounded like a crime was brought to my attention. I have no idea what the uniformed coppers did. They didn't deal with crime. Everything from a stolen bicycle to the theft of cash from an electricity meter ended up in my tray. Oh, and bestiality. Yes, I said bestiality. These were rural parts of Hampshire. I soon learned that it wasn't unheard-of for a man to release his sexual frustrations by coupling with a cow. I also learned that the modus operandi involved the use of a stool for the man to stand on. This was a far cry from my recent undercover days in Wales. I was slowly going mad.

There was a little respite from the sheer boredom of Tadley on the horizon. Whitchurch, about eight miles away, had a murder to deal with. It was a welcome relief and it was especially pleasing to work with Detective Chief Inspector. He was a gentleman of the old school. He was also a wise old detective and I learned from him.

The murder was typical in that most murder victims know their attackers. This was no different. The boyfriend was soon arrested and made a full confession. These were the days before the Crown Prosecution Service came along. Harry Dawson, a solicitor, was the appointed police prosecutor for the Basingstoke police division. Harry was based at the magistrates' court in that town. Harry would need a Director of Prosecutions (DPP) file. It was then a rule that before a prosecution for all serious crime, including murder, a DPP file needed preparing. It was sent to the Director of Public Prosecutions, a senior government lawyer. The compilation of a DPP file was the subject of much mystique within CID circles. It was common to hear one detective asking another, 'Have you done a DPP file yet?' It was uttered in whispered tones as if discussing a deep secret.

The DCI showed me how to put together a DPP file. He must have done a hundred in his time. Now nearing retirement, he appeared keen to show me the ropes. As he was a most approachable man, I asked him why he was taking the trouble to unravel the secrets of the DPP file for me. I was taken aback by what he told me.

'You are being watched.'

'Who by?'

'Tanky and other bosses to see if you are ready to be a Detective Sergeant.'

'Okay,' is all I could say.

'That's why I'm showing you how to do this.' He pointed to the pile of witness statements. Then there was another pile of photographs of the deceased. Paperclips, treasury tags and manila folders littered the desk in front of us.

'Promotion board' is the term used to describe the promotion application interview in Hampshire. Following my encouraging discussion with the DCI, I prepared to attend my second board. I had attended my first board while still in uniform at Basingstoke. That was shortly after my transfer from Merseyside. I wasn't impressed on that first occasion. I was asked if I was violent! The senior officer was referring to an unfounded complaint of assault made against me. I was then a 19-year-old rookie serving in the outskirts of Manchester.

I was also unimpressed at the second board. Many questions were posed about my role undercover in Wales. But it was clear to me I had to play along with the rules of their game. Under no circumstances was I permitted to talk about drug-taking. That was made abundantly clear.

The questions started with a long rambling preamble such as, 'We know that you would not have taken drugs but …'

It was farcical! Why ask a question if they didn't want a truthful answer? Typical internal police bullshit! They also showed me an appraisal report signed by Detective Chief Superintendent Holdaway. The content was fine but it was all about someone called 'Bennett'. Tanky couldn't even spell my name.

It was frustrating. Despite that, I had a glimmer of hope. I hoped for a promotion to keep me motivated during my banishment to Tadley. Working there was depressing and it seemed to me like a perverse punishment posting. It didn't stop me from drinking far too much. I wasn't quite drinking to the level I had while undercover in Llanddewi Brefi but it was still copious amounts and a regular nightly occurrence.

There wasn't a decent pub in Tadley and, in any case, I was not a solo drinker. I enjoyed the company of others.

## TWENTY-FIVE

There was a pub opposite the police station in Basingstoke run by a fellow Lancastrian. It was handy so it was used by both uniform and detectives from Basingstoke police station. I would start a session in there at about seven o'clock. Sometimes, I would have had enough to drink by midnight and drove home. Other nights, usually with a willing colleague, I would carry on drinking in the local night clubs. On one occasion, I drove to Bournemouth to go clubbing. Wherever I chose to drink, there was never a shortage of people wanting to hear all about my undercover exploits on Operation Julie. They were often disappointed, as most times I did not desire to talk about it. I felt that they would not have understood and, in any case, I was bottling up my innermost thoughts and feelings. I did write at the beginning of this book what I was describing as to what went on inside my head was with 'the benefit of hindsight'. It took many years to work my way through the myriad of thoughts.

The evening of 25 May 1977, was one occasion when I decided to stay home. It was the European Cup Final in Rome between Liverpool v. Borussia Monchengladbach and I wasn't going to miss that for all the tea in China. Settling down to watch it, I was aware of a buzzing sound in my ear. It was Jan, my now second wife, nagging! I thought, *What a time to start!* She persisted and, even after I had yelled at her, she continued. I'd had enough. The stresses of undercover and the frustrations of Tadley boiled over. I saw red and threw some plates against the wall, smashing them to pieces.

'I'm off to watch the match in peace,' I said before I stormed off, grabbing my car keys as I went. I watched the whole game, and Liverpool's win, from the pub. I rolled home again at about four the following morning. The end was nigh for my second marriage.

## TWENTY-SIX

# 124 YEARS' JAIL

The sentencing of all the Operation Julie defendants took place at Bristol Crown Court on 8 March 1978. Mr Justice Park, a judge of the High Court, handed out a total of 124 years' imprisonment on 15 defendants. Sentences totalling 46 years had earlier been passed down on 14 other defendants. More than a hundred others had been dealt with at the lower courts. They were for relatively minor offences but had been caught up in the final casting of the net in the countrywide Operation Julie finale. Kemp and Todd were each sentenced to 13 years' imprisonment. The maximum sentence at that time was 14 years.

There was a news frenzy following the sentencing. Every newspaper in the land carried photographs of the conspirators and the Julie team. Many also had Eric and me as a separate feature. Many more column inches were devoted to the success of Operation Julie. That night, and for the first time ever, the BBC extended its usual 30-minute evening news bulletin. Instead, it had an hour-long programme. It was filled with a documentary-like coverage of the Julie story. It was crazy! It did not abate for some considerable time.

The next fillip in the news coverage followed the same judge's commendation. It was addressed to all the Operation Julie squad members. On 10 March, the courtroom was packed with squad members, the press, and the public to hear what Mr Justice Park had to say:

> *I had hoped to complete my duties in this case by today but various events have prevented me from doing this, but I can delay no longer the public expression of my admiration of everything about Operation Julie. Over the last few days the press and the television have rightly given tremendous coverage to the amazing detective work that led to these arrests, and to the extreme hardship endured by many police officers involved in it; I have learned from various sources and from the Chief Constable of Avon and Somerset, who I suppose you can rely on as a reliable source, many things which of course were not disclosed in the committal documents.*
>
> *I refer particularly to the extreme hardship endured by the police officers in that operation. I refer to the long separation of police officers from their families and the need for total secrecy about the reasons for those separations and the consequent misunderstandings and strain which I hear some family relationships underwent.*
>
> *And so, these police officers and these police activities required of the police officers sacrifices of the kind which policemen and policewomen, along with other members of*

> *the public, are expected to endure only in wartime, never in peacetime.*
>
> *I myself was very greatly impressed by the fairness and candour with which all the police officers who had to give evidence in this court gave that evidence. Now, may I turn aside and pay tribute to all those officers and others who have had the duty of guarding, arranging and finding when required the numerous exhibits in this case. That was a gigantic undertaking in itself and in my view as successfully accomplished as Operation Julie. And so, Mr. Kennedy [counsel for the prosecution] I am proud to be the judge who, on behalf of the public finds, himself entitled to say that every officer concerned with Operation Julie must be most highly commended. Those words don't really seem adequate. I was pleased to see that they had their photograph in* The Times *newspaper this morning and I hope that they all think that photograph does them justice.*

Many of the London media had camped in various Bristol hotels for the days between sentencing and the judge's commendation hearing. I stayed at Eric's home so as not to miss any of the hullabaloo and it was a welcome distraction from Tadley.

As Eric and I were two of the undercover detectives, we were popular with a section of the media. Particularly with one vivacious and voluptuous female journalist. She listened to our story with rapture, taking down copious notes. It was now about 3pm and she had completed her note-taking. She was in no rush to file her copy as she worked for a weekly journal that featured sensationalist stories.

Like many professions, journalists have a penchant for boozing. Eric and Jan had other things to attend to and left the curvy blonde journo alone with me. She seemed turned on by meeting a real undercover officer and wanted to spend more time with me. No problem – this was a better prospect than a tedious drive home along the M4 Motorway. We retired to her hotel room. It was a threesome – me, her and Johnnie Walker! I left after giving her a scoop!

• • •

The next night, Eric, his wife, Jan, and I went to dinner with Colin Wills, the showbiz editor of the *Daily Mirror*. It was a drunken night spent in a steak house close to Bristol Crown Court. Wills paid for everything in return for our story. He was good company and we were often raucously laughing at the many jokes exchanged between us. That annoyed a group of people in there but I wasn't aware of that until I decided it was time to pee.

I wandered off to find the men's urinals but found a queue. I needed to go so I went out into the street by way of the restaurant front door. As I made my way through the front door, the same group we had seemed to annoy were blocking the exit. In polite tones, I asked them to make way. They grudgingly obliged but threw a few ribald comments in my direction. They seemed to know who I was. No surprise there. My picture had appeared in every newspaper in the country. I ignored them.

A piece of waste ground stood about 30 yards away. It was perfect. I urinated to my heart's content and in peace, out of sight of the street. All was well in my world. On my return to the steak house, the group was still in the small vestibule on the inside of the front door. It was one of those large heavy framed solid wood doors with the automatic closer fixed to the top on the inside. It took a little effort to push it open owing to the combined weight of the frame and glass.

As I did so, three burly members of this obstructive group pushed the door closed. The main problem with this was that my hand was still between the door and the adjoining fixed frame. My hand was jammed in a tiny gap between the door and its frame. I was drunk but I could feel pain. It was a dull pain, but pain nonetheless. The alcohol anaesthetised the pain. I put my shoulder to the door. To no avail, as the three gorillas on the other side were using their combined strength to entrap my hand. They were laughing at me, and seemingly enjoying it.

I have no idea even now why I didn't get mad and swear at them. Instead, I went into a zone of my own creation. It was a case of mind over matter. I was not allowing my body to experience pain. My zone kept me calm and it surprised me. My calmness and silence disturbed them. I could see they were starting to shuffle. They became uneasy.

My thoughts turned toward Eric and rescue. *Where are you when I need you?* reverberated through my head. A further thought crashed into my head, *Okay, no Eric. But someone will want to come out through that door soon.* No one did.

The self-induced zone was becoming harder to perpetuate. My hand was throbbing. I summoned up all my powers of serenity but paradoxically mouthed through the glass at my tormentors, 'I will fucking kill all of you!' PC Lake came to mind at that moment. Once again, I did mean what I said. The uneasiness of my captors transformed into a panic. They ran and disappeared inside the restaurant with its many rooms and booths. I had no intention of seeking them out.

As I sat down beside Eric, Jan and Colin Wills, they enquired what had taken me so long. A one-word reply. 'Nothing'.

Jan, it's always the women who are perceptive, asked if I was okay. Using short syllables, I assured her I was fine. No one noticed that my hand had swollen to twice its normal size. Five minutes later, I decided to do something. I had no idea what and had no plan. I left the company and made for the front door. There was no sign of the gorillas. It seemed like a good idea to pee again, so returning to my spot on the wasteland, I relieved myself once more.

This parcel of waste ground was in darkness. I walked up as far as the adjoining building. I stopped at its corner where it turned at right angles to follow the street building line. I was still in darkness but I was able to see the illuminated street outside the steak house. There were some cars, including Eric's, parked in the street. They were on the opposite side to the restaurant owing to parking restrictions.

Still without any plan, I decided to wait and watch from my covert position.

*There they are!* I shouted in silence to myself.

A group of about seven men walked from the steak house to a car. The gorillas were among them. It was their turn to be noisy. I couldn't hear what they were laughing at but I imagined it was me. Their noise covered my approach as I ran toward them. One man opened the boot of the parked car using a key and I saw he was taking hold of a long jack handle. He turned and swung it at me. Undeterred and focused, I hit him first. I kneed him in the balls. He fell to the ground groaning, the jack handle clattering beside him. Another swung a fist at me and missed. My uppercut connected with his jaw. *Two down!* Two others came at me cussing on their approach. I picked up the jack handle. One aimed a kick, which caught me on my thigh. The other swung a haymaker but as he did so, I crashed the jack handle into his left upper arm. He whelped like a puppy, turned and ran away.

Another two then attacked me, aiming kicks and throwing punches. I fended off most of them. Then I felt my legs give way. One of my attackers had kicked me from behind. I fell to the ground. It was then I became aware of Eric. He sat on top of me. I was trying to get up to fight some more. Eric was too heavy and too strong. He later told me he was afraid

I was going to do some real damage to these guys because I was out of control. He didn't recognise me as the same man he had worked with undercover.

I am led to believe that at this point I broke down and sobbed uncontrollably. My recollection of that is sketchy. I recall Eric pinning me down and feeling distraught. Eric tells me that I told him all about a hard upbringing in Liverpool. That makes sense. I have a revulsion toward bullies. I was the subject of bullying at school in Liverpool because I was the son of a policeman. It was not until I was 17 years old that I found out I was capable of fighting fire with fire. It was when my younger brother was bullied at school. I flattened his tormentor and it felt good.

It did feel good. I am not proud of the capacity for violence. Normally, I am placid and laid back. I am not one for pointing fingers at the parents when trying to lay blame for the acts of their children. Yet it is arguable that parents can and do leave mental scars on their children. In most cases, it is entirely an unintentional consequence. My vivid mental scar is a confrontation outside my Liverpool home when I was 11. I had been watching my father fix his car at the front of our home. A group of local bullies walked by, shouting at me to come and fight. No way! One was a kid who, a few years later transfixed another kid to a tree at school by sticking a knife through his hand. He was the one shouting at me. My father urged me to go and punch him. I refused. My father didn't let it go. Instead, he remonstrated with me for being "weak." A double humiliation, one by the bully and another by my father.

That night in Bristol took me back to younger days. The guys who trapped my hand in the door had no idea what they were tapping into. There are parts of me that I do not like. One of them is a fury that can be released against perceived injustice and bullying. It lies in stark contrast to a normally placid guy. Perhaps that is what Jan, Eric's partner, meant when she described me as having a 'brooding undercurrent'.

Some weeks later, I learned that some of this group had lodged an official complaint against me. Again, they were able to identify me because of the extensive media coverage. I was interviewed under caution by a police superintendent. He told me I was being investigated about a complaint of causing grievous bodily harm. That is a serious charge. It was said that I had broken someone's jaw. A key part of that caution is the part about not being obliged to say anything. I kept silent. I answered no questions and declined to make a statement. Some months later, I was notified that there would be no further proceedings against me. In my eyes, justice was done.

That night at the Bristol steak house was when I snapped. Partly because of my early Liverpool experiences of bullying. And it was partly a manifestation of the strains of undercover work.

Hindsight is a wonderful thing. It was a time I would have benefitted from counselling. Who knows how things may have turned out?

## TWENTY-SEVEN

# FIFTEEN PINTS

Promotion to Detective Sergeant and a transfer to Farnborough kept my interest in a police career going, at least for a while. I was supervising a half dozen detectives and their workload. I found it all too easy and soon lacked focus and a challenge. I was de facto the boss. I was kind of supervised by a Detective Inspector based at nearby Aldershot. That British Army garrison town housed the Aldershot Police HQ. That was where the boss, the Detective Chief Inspector had his office. My team and I rarely saw him or the DI, an affable but hapless Irishman.

Aldershot also accommodated the Special Investigation Branch (SIB) of the Military Police. We worked in tandem with them in cases involving military personnel or property. The trouble was they had an excellent mess. As guest police officers, it was fine to have a mess bill – a drinks tab paid up at the end of every month. The SIB mess also served excellent curries. They were two good reasons I enjoyed my frequent visits there.

The drinking sessions carried on unabated. Back in my day, the life of a detective involved drinking copious amounts of beer. As a rookie 21-year-old detective in Kirkby,

Merseyside, it amazed me how the likes of Ian Dodd, one of my first Detective Sergeants, could sup 15 pints of beer in one session. He was still sharp at work the next morning.

As an impressionable callow youth, I aspired to reach those benchmarks. I could manage 12, but Doddy's benchmark of 15 was out of reach -- and retch! Heavy drinking and detectives were synonymous. It was part of the CID culture to work a split shift day. Most of us returned to the office every evening at about seven o'clock. We would mostly sit at our office desk attending to outstanding paperwork until about nine o'clock. Then, it was half-a-brick time. An imaginary half-brick was tossed in the air. If it stayed airborne, we would all go home. If it crashed to earth, then we would split up into pairs to go boozing. The object was to meet contacts old and new and, of course, gather information.

The boozing mostly ended up in social chat and only on the odd occasion did someone want to talk in confidence, to grass on someone.

Farnborough was no different. The CID office there, now under my wing, had the same work ethic – work hard, play hard. I had willing accomplices in the play-hard category: the late Peter Strickland, who became a close friend; Graham Hoyle; and a young Bob Duncan.

Graham was a fellow Lancastrian. We once educated the uniform shift in the art of how to cook and eat a real Lancashire black pudding from Bury. On his return from a trip to his native roots, Graham proudly produced some

Bury black pudding. It wasn't the type one found in the stores of southern England. They were the salami-like sausages.

These real puds resembled the shape of a fist. My brother, when he was a child, called them boxing gloves. They were tied together with string. Graham took them upstairs to the canteen at Farnborough Police Station and filled a pan with water. Setting the pan on the stovetop he waited for the black puddings to boil, then let them simmer for about five minutes. The result was a gourmand's delight. The insides are so tasty and crumbly in texture. A little English mustard is a perfect accompaniment. The boys in uniform on their refreshments break were amazed. They had seen nothing like it before and the ones who tasted it were also impressed.

Our regular boozing haunts, besides the SIB mess, were the Tumbledown Dick and a hotel in Queens Road. The hotel was owned and run by a strange gay guy, John. Drunken escapades were a regular feature of working life in Farnborough. There had been a spate of thefts in a private locker room area reserved for employees at a large upmarket hotel. Bob Duncan and I investigated.

We spent some 5-6 hours over an inquiry that should have taken one hour. The attraction? Free booze and sandwiches. I left at about one in the morning. CID in Hampshire at that time was using Minis with no markings, but with a VHF radio set fitted.

I was driving along the main road toward Farnborough Police Station when we heard a chase was going on. It involved about ten police cars in pursuit of a suspected stolen car. This pursuit started in neighbouring Surrey. The Renault estate car failed to stop when requested. We heard on the radio that the convoy was heading in our direction. A few minutes later, I saw the stolen car travelling toward us at high speed. The flashing lights of at least six Surrey police cars were in hot pursuit. I told Bob to hold tight.

Physics was not my strongest subject at school. But I did know, through my love of sport, that even the slightest nudge from the little guy can bring down the mighty. My befuddled drunken thinking told me this would also apply in our given situation. I yanked sharply on the steering wheel at the moment we were almost level with the front of the Renault. I flicked it and straightened up the wheel. It worked! I saw in my rear-view mirror that the offender had skidded and ended up stationary at the side of the road. The chase had concluded. No one had been hurt.

One of the uniformed chasing officers approached us as we still sat in the CID Mini. 'You okay?'

'We're fine,' I flashed my warrant card. I had started to shake a little.

'You sure you're okay?'

'Fine thanks. Shaken but not stirred.'

'Great piece of driving, by the way.'

'Thanks. We'll make a statement tomorrow and fax it over to you. We're dog-tired and need some kip.'

Thankfully, he agreed to that idea, as the last thing I needed was to run the risk of a breathalyser test.

• • •

Making off without payment is a criminal offence. It was introduced in the Theft Act of 1968 to cater to a situation where people consumed a meal and made off without payment. Most people call that "doing a runner." Before, under the old Larceny Act, there had been difficulties. There existed a plethora of legal cases leading to problems in the prosecution of runners.

The CID drinking sessions were sometimes interrupted by Indian or Chinese restaurant meals. The session may have been interrupted, but not the drinking. The beer still flowed before, during and after the meal. A detective colleague and I went to an Aldershot Chinese restaurant. We both enjoyed the meal and the beers. I went for a pee, telling my junior colleague we would split the bill on my return. I sat at our table on my return, and waited, waited and ... waited. He had gone ... vanished, and no money was left on the table.

My mentality had undergone a sea change during and after my undercover work. I was now a risk-taker extraordinaire and revelled in it. Peers perceived me as bold and held me in high regard. They were in awe of what I had experienced during Operation Julie. The risk-taking had become an adrenaline junkie's substitute for the real thrill of working deep undercover.

I had worked out that I had no money to pay the bill that lay on the table in front of me. I knew that because I had a quick look in my wallet and the change in my pocket before I left the urinals. I made my mind up. There was a Chinese waiter stationed on the door acting as both a guard and welcomer. I bided my time and bolted as soon as he deserted his post.

Running at full tilt into the street, I became aware of two things. The Chinese waiter was now pursuing me, waving a large chopping blade in circles above his head. I also caught a glimpse of my colleague. He was sat in the parked CID Mini outside the restaurant. I heard him roaring with laughter, no doubt at the sight of an irate, knife-wielding waiter chasing his Detective Sergeant!

Running fast was not an issue for me in those days. It helped to know that, if caught, I was going to be rushed to hospital with a gaping wound in my head. The prospect of arrest did not enter my head. I shook off the angry waiter and hid in a refuse dumpster behind some shops. I awoke there several hours later and walked the two miles back to the police station. I collected my car and drove home.

• • •

There were many lock-ins at the drinking holes I frequented. One of the regular lock-in spots was the Tumbledown Dick hotel. It was there I met Catherine. It became known as the 'zany night'. Peter Strickland and I were looking for a late drink when we got to the Tumbledown.

The front bar was empty so we went through to the large hall at the back. It had a bar, dance floor and raised stage at the far side. We were drinking for about four hours, staying until the early hours of the following morning. Catherine was with her friend Mary. Pete, Graham the landlord – and I went through the entire Buddy Holly jukebox playlist. We sang each note and every line to whichever song came on. The two girls joined in with gusto. I left that morning with Catherine and so began the start of a 30-year relationship.

I did have some sense of propriety. I did not get drunk during the day when I was working ... well, only once.

It was Christmas 1979 and the detective roster thinned down, which meant personnel could take turns at spending some time with family over the festive period. I was on duty with Pete Strickland on Christmas Eve. We visited an elderly lady who had reported a break-in at her home. On an examination of the crime scene, it was clear that her tale did not gel. Further chat with her revealed that she was in the early stages of dementia. I think she also needed someone to talk to, so we stayed for a while and listened. She knew it was Christmas Eve and offered us some whiskey. It was only about eleven in the morning, but we didn't want to offend her feelings.

At around one o'clock that afternoon, Peter and I left her home. The Bell's whisky bottle now empty. We now had the "taste." A small personal UHF radio kept us in touch with Farnborough Police Station. All was quiet, so we went to the Tumbledown for an all-afternoon session.

## TWENTY-SEVEN

Still in the Tumbledown, it was mid-evening when Peter Strickland returned from the toilets. Pete had the radio.

He said, 'Fuck me, Skip, they want us to go to a burglary down the road.'

The 'fuck me' meant that it was a hardship owing to the fact we were both rat-assed! Sucking on menthol and sucking in our breath, we went into the home that had been broken into that day. It was a mess. The thief had ransacked the rooms in the search for goods worth stealing.

The homeowners had been out at work. They finished late to finalise important tasks seeing it was Christmas Eve. They were understandably upset at the sight that greeted them on their return. Pete spotted a social security benefits payment book laying on the carpet. Curious, as the homeowners were a childless working couple, he asked if they had seen it before.

'No,' came the answer.

It belonged to the felon who had dropped it in his drunken befuddled state. Within the hour, we knocked on the suspect's door. There was no need to worry about the smell of alcohol on our breath any longer. The suspect opened his front door and the stench was reminiscent of a brewery. We were in good company!

Tommy confessed immediately. He pleaded with us to go for another beer before taking him to the police station. Using it as a bargaining chip, he added that he would make a full written confession at the nick. Peter glanced at me. I winked back at him and told Tommy that it was a good plan.

We knew we would have to take him to the custody suite at Aldershot. Farnborough nick was running on a skeleton crew over Christmas. The drive to Aldershot would entail passing close to the hotel run by the strange gay guy. It was now late and, to be sure of keeping our side of the bargain with Tommy, it seemed best to go to the hotel. There were no lights on at the front of the hotel, so Pete went to the back and rang the bell several times. This was urgent police business.

John answered and opened the back door, which revealed a glimpse of the filthy kitchen area. He appeared flustered and a little angry. Pete explained to him what was afoot and told him the truth. John became animated.

He lisped in a most dramatic fashion, 'How exciting!' At the same time, he threw a hand to his sweaty forehead in true diva style.

We arrived at the grey concrete block of Aldershot Police Station after several beers and an interesting chat with Tommy. He was as good as his word and made a full confession in writing.

## TWENTY-EIGHT

# CHIEF'S COMMENDATION

A festering discontent started to ferment in my head. I was thrilled to hear and read the comments of Mr Justice Park in his commendation of all the officers involved in the Operation Julie investigation. I had started to compile a scrapbook of all the press cuttings I could lay my hands on in the wake of the sentencing. Pride of place was a transcript of the judge's commendation and a letter from the Director of Public Prosecutions (DPP) to the Hampshire Chief Constable.

The letter from the DPP repeated the text of the learned judge's comments but added:

> *The officers in your force to whom this applies were Detective Sergeant 870 Peter Spencer and Detective Constable 708 Stephen Bentley.*
>
> *As you will know, this most major investigation, unique in scope and character, was conceived and executed with complete success.*

I eventually received a copy of this letter in the internal mail. In the top right-hand corner, there was a cursory handwritten note from the Assistant Chief Constable 'O' (Operations):

> HQ Drugs – Inform officers – then to 'P' for attachment to personal files.

'P' means the Personnel Department.

A further letter was received by the Hampshire Chief Constable on 28 March 1978, from the Chief Constable of Wiltshire. It again contained the judge's sentencing remarks. It enclosed a copy of a letter from a Wiltshire-based defence solicitor, the lawyer who had represented Russ Spenceley. In it he commended the work of the Operation Julie team despite being in the opposing team.

Once more there was a cursory handwritten note on the letter marking it for my "information and retention." These notifications appeared to be dealt with in a perfunctory, impersonal and dismissive manner. It hurt.

I became convinced I was bound to receive a Chief's Commendation because of my prominent undercover role in the investigation and the sheer weight of nationwide publicity. After all, Mr Justice Park, a High Court Judge of England and Wales, had said that we 'must be highly commended'. I am still waiting.

A Chief's commendation would have meant the world to me. My father had served for many years with distinction in the Liverpool City Police and the Dorset Police. He had received at least two Chief Constable's commendations during his time in Liverpool. He was proud of them and would often show me the books he was presented with at the ceremony to mark the distinction. Despite difficulties in the relationship with my father, I was proud of his achievements. I was proud of his tenacity and physical courage in his dealings with violent criminals. Those attributes led to his commendations. In no small measure, they led me to my own career in the police force.

I became anxious as the weeks and months passed by that my own Chief's commendation was nowhere in sight. I wished to announce to my father that I had emulated him. The absence of official recognition became a monkey on my back. I was unable to shake it off. In a discussion with my father, at the time still a serving Chief Superintendent in Dorset, he also found it incredible that no commendation was forthcoming. He went on to give me some comfort. He told me that he marvelled at what I had experienced and it far surpassed anything he had ever done. Even so, it was like a piece of grit in my shoe. It was there and I was unable to shift it. I was astute enough to know that commendations like this were not thrown about confetti-style, but …

Matters got worse when I saw that Greenslade was awarded a Queen's Police Medal in H.M. Queen Elizabeth's Honours List in 1978. This is the highest award that a serving police officer can achieve. It is only awarded for service with distinction. At least there was one police officer connected to Operation Julie who received a gong! It's just a pity that it was possibly gained through false pretences. That's just my opinion. I believe it had all to do with his placement on top of the Operation Julie command structure to spy on Lee on behalf of the Establishment. As far as I am concerned Greenslade was a glory hunter.

There was no better example of this than just after all the conspirators had been first locked up in cells at Swindon Police Station. It had been a long day and Lee had called the team together for a well-earned celebratory drink. Interviews could wait for the following day. Not Greenslade! He announced that he was going to see all the conspirators one by one. This was a crazy thing to do. Lee had already notified us of the interview teams. We knew who was going to interview which prisoner. These interview teams had done their homework. Each team prepared a dossier on each prisoner in preparation for the interview. Greenslade threatened to ruin all the well-laid plans by his stupidity. I am convinced that he envisaged glory. I believe he was conceited enough to think each prisoner would, in turn, make a full confession to the glory hunter! That was typical of the man. I described him as an idiot earlier in this book and I do not retract the use of that word.

I am now over the bitter disappointment of not receiving any kind of official recognition. Or am I? I believed I was. Yet, as I pore over the judge's words it beggars belief that my former bosses chose to ignore him. In retrospect, I believe it was one factor behind my depressive illness. There are few things worse than making sacrifices and endangering your health and then not being recognised. I used to wonder if

I would have received the accolade of a CC's commendation if I had been a member of the Freemasons, the secretive group that permeated the force.

Resignations from former members of the Operation Julie team were piling up. They included:

- Eric Wright
- Martyn Pritchard
- Dick Lee
- John McWalter
- Alan Buxton

This was a serious loss of detective talent. Most of them cited the lack of foresight in not permitting Operation Julie to continue. They believed it should be set up as an embryo National Drug Squad. They believed in it enough to fall on their own swords. The idea of a national drugs squad was conceived but never went full term, never mind born. *The Times* took up the cudgel to use its influence within the Establishment but to no avail.

The news of these resignations and the lack of personal internal official recognition played on my mind. It unsettled me. It was a further step closer to my own decision about my future. And a not-insignificant factor in my future acute depression.

• • •

Back to the debauchery. The drinking carried on unabated in my role as Detective Sergeant at Farnborough. It was now fuelled by resentment toward my senior officers and contempt for some of those who were allegedly supervising me. The tedium of the office duties associated with my new supervisory role was numbing. I wanted action! Now!

The best moments of my role as a Detective Sergeant were in action mode, particularly when showcasing my thief-taking abilities to junior detectives. It proved to myself that I still had the knack. Like undercover skills, the knack cannot be taught. It is intuition. Bob Duncan and I attended the scene of a burglary at a tyre store. Tyres to the value of about £10,000 (in today's money, at least £50,000) had been stolen in an overnight raid. It was clear that the thieves used a truck of some description.

Leaving the tyre warehouse about 9.30am, I said to Bob, 'We'll go have a sniff around after a bacon sarnie'.

Bob was not yet an official detective. He was known as a 'CID Aide'. Other forces call them 'Temporary DC's'. He was there for assessment and evaluation as a potential detective. He did okay, ending up as a Detective Superintendent before his retirement. I hope he learned the good bits from me and quickly jettisoned some of my excesses! I talked him through my idea during our sandwiches and mugs of steaming tea.

'I bet it was travellers.'

There was a large community of Irish travellers in the area and some had earned a reputation for stealing. The area to the south and east of Aldershot was where they tended to congregate. That is the area where we drove to on leaving the café.

As we drove down a quiet road surrounded by council houses, I spotted four travellers. They were up to no good and I knew they were, don't ask me how; I have no idea, but I was right. They were looking about them for no reason that I could discern. Then I realised that a parked car had driven them to that street. I didn't see them get out of it; again, I just knew.

We watched the four men and followed them as they turned a corner into an adjacent street. They were still walking. They walked about a hundred yards until they stopped at an 18-tonne truck. Once again looking all about, they climbed into the truck's cab. I slewed our CID Mini in front of the truck and both Bob and I alighted.

I showed my ID and asked the driver, 'Whose is the truck?'

A typical Irish accent boomed back, 'It's me mate's'.

All four were nervous.

'No problem if I take a look in the back? Bob, hold on to these,' and handed him the keys from the ignition.

We saw two brand-new tyres in the back of the truck. There were some sticky labels strewn across the floor. The type that would be affixed to a new tyre.

I returned to the driver and the rest of the crew. I told them they were being arrested on suspicion of theft of a large number of tyres. After caution, one started to say, 'On my mother's life and on the life of ...'

'I was wondering how long it was going to take for one of you to come out with that crap!'

I wish I had a quid for every time I heard someone with Irish blood swearing to the truth over the lives of their mothers and babies!

We used our UHF personal radio to call up a van and they were carted off to Aldershot Police Station. The travellers were waiting for us in the custody suite when Bob and I arrived. I let Bob go through the routine of justifying to the custody sergeant the reason for their arrest and subsequent detention. Norman Green was listening from the back of the sparsely furnished booking-in area. The suspects were led off to the cell as Green spoke to me. He had recently been installed as the new Divisional Chief promoted from Detective. Supt. at HQ ops. He was a detective through and through but this last promotion out of plainclothes was a career move.

'What you got against them, Steve?'

'Fuck all, really! Just a hunch.'

'You better get a cough then,' was the brief observation as he walked away and back to his ivory tower office.

'Cough' is a detective's slang for admission, a confession. Whether you are called a detective, a 'D', or a 'jack', a 'cough' was a badge of honour. Only the best Ds or jacks achieved high confession rates. Interrogation, unlike undercover work, was a skill that could be taught. And I was taught by a master on my Home Office Detective Training Course in Preston. None other than Joe Mounsey, who had gained fame thanks to his involvement in the Moors Murders case, and the subsequent arrests and convictions of Ian Brady and Myra Hindley in the 1960s.

These were pre-Police and Criminal Evidence Procedure Act (PACE) days, and there was no audio recording of interviews. There were not the same safeguards in place introduced by PACE in 1984. Nothing untoward was said or done to the four travellers. Two confessed to their part in the theft of the tyres and we recovered all the stolen tyres. I can assure you that the fact that two of them were swiftly released had no bearing on the remaining pair deciding to admit it all! The cynics among you may have raised an eyebrow on learning that it was the sons who were released. The fathers decided to accept all responsibility for the crime.

## TWENTY-NINE

# HOUSE ARREST

The tyre incident was a welcome piece of the action. There were not enough of them. I detested paperwork and my part in collating daily crime statistics. They were the basis of my daily report to my divisional CID boss every single morning. He was a stickler for detail and treated stats like a holy commandment. He was in a spiritual state of grace once he had collected his daily stat reports. Then he would communicate the contents to HQ. Horses for courses, I guess.

My detestation of paperwork almost led to my undoing. The work I had done on the murder case while a DC at Tadley came back to bite my arse. My former boss had travelled over to Aldershot to see me and others in that Division. He came to see those detectives involved in his murder investigation. The murder trial date was looming and my old boss was keen to do a "pocketbook check." That was in case there was a contested trial where the defendant maintained a plea of not guilty. At any trial, police witnesses would use their pocket notebooks to refresh the memory.

The police witness first needs the permission of the court. The ritual in court usually followed these lines:

> OFFICER *(in response to an early question from prosecuting counsel)*: May I refer to my pocketbook, Your Honour?
>
> JUDGE: When did you make the notes?
>
> OFFICER: At ABC time on XYZ date.
>
> JUDGE *(asking a leading question)*: Were the events still fresh in your mind at the time of making the notes?

That was always a rhetorical question. Never did I hear an answer in the negative.

Sometimes a rookie officer would cause a hoot of laughter in court. If it was their first trial at a court higher than the lowly local magistrates' court, then you may have heard something like this:

> PROSECUTING COUNSEL: Officer, please introduce yourself to the members of the jury.
>
> ROOKIE OFFICER: May I please refer to my notebook?

It was no joke when I learned of the purpose of my former boss's visit. He was being thorough. Ensuring that all potential police witnesses were trial-ready. That they had possession of a notebook complete with relevant evidence. I had nothing in any notebook!

My evidence, if I was called to give it, was minor. I knew it was best to come clean with my governor. I explained to him that my evidence was in the signed witness statements that I had made. They were part of the case papers. The defence lawyers, both counsel and solicitor, would read those statements. The defendant would also read them. It was they who decided whether to call me to challenge my evidence or accept it. In the latter case, it would be read out to the jury by prosecuting counsel. The defence had not indicated anything yet. I had never seen my former boss mad before. His usual calm demeanour had disappeared. He conferred with an old buddy who was now my current Detective Chief Inspector and came up with a plan.

They arranged it so I was a prisoner under house arrest in a now-empty CID office at Aldershot Police Station. There was a guard on the door. He had instructions to bring me a pint of beer from the top floor social club on the hour, every hour until I had finished my task. It took me about five hours to transcribe the contents of my statements by hand into two pocket notebooks. I completed it about 11.30pm and rushed to the social club bar in time for last orders. I ordered three more pints of beer and swallowed them in no time at all. My old boss was still there, and I inquired if anything else was to happen to me.

'I may have to file a disciplinary report.'

'Okay guv, I understand. What's likely to happen?'

'You might have to go to HQ and be disciplined.'

'Oh, fuck! Really?'

'Yes. But don't worry.'

'What do you mean?'

'Just remember this – they can't make you pregnant!'

That's a line I have always recalled when facing a worrying situation. It makes me smile. Thank you, governor.

In my days, detectives had two notebooks. One was the pocket type and identical to those carried by their uniformed counterparts. The other was specific to CID. It was larger, and known as a desk diary. Before computerisation, a detective noted his daily activities in that diary. New blank pocketbooks and diaries were kept under lock and key. It was possible for any detective to access as many new pocketbooks or diaries as he wished. Only as recently as 2013 did I burn both a pocketbook and desk diary. They were both blank and never used. I no longer have evidence of the practice then of manipulating an entry or entries into the record. This practice ceased with the introduction of time stamps.

The newspapers still carried the odd article about Operation Julie. They included stories about the seizure of assets, particularly involving cash in Swiss bank accounts. ITV also made a film for TV and it was aired with a fanfare of accompanying publicity. They were all reminders of a time etched into my soul. My alter ego Steve Jackson was still a living, breathing part of me.

My relationship with Catherine had become serious. Just before the Christmas of 1979, I decided to abandon my marital home in Basingstoke. It was time to move in with Catherine in Farnborough. I was spending more time at her home before then and rarely did I spend a night in Basingstoke. I drove to the first-floor flat I was buying in Basingstoke and threw some clothes in black plastic bags. Jan ran out of the flat following me to my car. She was distraught and pleaded with me to stay. I felt bad in ignoring her as I never meant to hurt anyone in my life. It's a terrible reflection on me, and humanity, that we are capable of giving so much happiness and misery to the same person. While writing this book, Paul, Jan's son, contacted me. It was good to hear from him, but I was saddened to learn of his mother's premature death.

I had only been at Catherine's for a few weeks when she learned that her husband had returned from Poland. He was working on a construction site there. He had a Polish girlfriend out there and later married her. He scared Catherine. She decided to move to her parents' empty flat in Sevenoaks for the Christmas period. I took some leave and joined her and her children.

It was shortly before that Christmas that Norman Green paid us a visit. It was a futile attempt to force me to return to work. It was over that festive period that I decided I'd had enough of the police force.

I was now in a relationship I felt was going to work out. I needed that stability in my life after the highs of my undercover days. The thought of a forced separation was unbearable. An 80-mile, round trip commute was not workable. The shift patterns as a uniformed Sergeant would be problematic. I felt it would be too tiring to commute every day. In any event, I felt I was being punished for falling in love and leaving my wife for Catherine. Whichever way I looked at it, being sent back to uniform duties was a punishment. *How dare they? What had my private life to do with the police force? Nothing!* Believe me – that's how it was back then, incredible as it may seem in the twenty-first century!

This was a police force that had refused to give me any kind of official recognition of my sacrifices when undercover. No police officer knew how depressed I was. No one offered me any kind of counselling to help me out of my depression. I guess these days my state of mind would have been labelled as a Post-Traumatic Stress Disorder[13].

I was also wracked with guilt about deceiving Smiles. I considered him to be a good friend. I had no one to talk to about my feelings or thoughts. I was as down as down could be. I didn't give a fuck about the future. I didn't give a fuck about my career. I didn't give a fuck about throwing away lucrative pension entitlements. I just didn't give a fuck!

The heavy drinking was constant. I was reckless. One of my other regular watering holes was a private club in Farnborough owned and run by a likeable Irish building contractor. Most Friday and Saturday nights would see me drinking to excess in his club. So much so on one occasion that I forced my way out of the car park in my own car. On leaving for the night, I found my exit blocked by several cars.

I continually switched between first and reverse gears, shunting all out of my way until I had made a gap. I had access to cannabis and was still smoking it on a regular basis. It was a downward spiral and the thought of donning a uniform again was out of the question.

'I am a detective!' I would scream at the mirror.

In a state of despair, I concluded that I was to hand in my resignation.

I did not return to work. I consulted a doctor and he agreed I was in no fit mental state to work. He referred me to a psychiatrist at a local hospital. I made an appointment but failed to attend. I didn't give a fuck!

# THIRTY

# RESIGNATION

I am back in the corridor near the office of the Deputy Chief Constable at Police HQ in Winchester. I had just stormed out of the police doctor's office after telling him he was not qualified to have an opinion on my fitness to work.

The thought train continued ... *Maybe heads are going to roll?*

I swear I saw disembodied heads rolling along the corridor. I laughed out loud. *I'm for the high jump?*, popped my next thought. *Perhaps Fosbury-flopping would be a good way to enter the DCC's office?* These thoughts ran through my mind at the same time as I heard Procol Harum's 'A Whiter Shade of Pale' playing inside my head.

At that point, a lucidity returned. It became so clear what I had to do. I rose from the silent chair, walked to the lift and retraced my journey to the floor of the gods but in reverse. I knew I had made my decision. Fuck them all!

'Fuck you all!' was my unwritten resignation note.

I saw out my resignation period from my home in Farnborough. I wallowed in despair and depression for some time. It was difficult to motivate myself to do anything positive.

There was no work, no income for months in the wake of my resignation. I was not aware of any skill sets other than the detective's that I possessed. This situation compounded my deep depression. Finally, I found work as a double-glazing salesman in Aldershot. I walked there the first morning as I had no money for the bus fare.

By the end of 1980, I had success with an application for a post as an investigator. It was for the Hong Kong Police Anti-Corruption Commission. I was supplied with details of my accommodation in the colony. They also provided details of the local schools for Catherine's children. There was one proviso – we must be a married couple for us to travel and live in Hong Kong. We obliged.

About a month before our planned departure, I received a letter from a UK Government department in London. It informed me that the offer had been rescinded. Of course, it added the phrase 'with regret'. The English excel at politeness! And duplicity! I was furious and contacted anyone I thought could help. I spoke with a friendly and sympathetic former senior police officer. He told me someone who had never met me had "blackballed" me. *Fuck them all!*

I was an angry man now. I hated the police force and I hated all coppers. Even by my standards, I got steaming drunk early one Sunday evening. I staggered into a pub in the town centre of Weybridge, an upmarket snooty kind of place. Catherine and I had been living at another Weybridge pub managed by her brother, John. Earlier in the day, she and a friend had gone to the snooty place to escape the drunken antics of John and his guests. As she had been gone for some time, I set off to find her. She gave me a nasty look as I walked into the pub. It was a look that made me feel like a worthless piece of shit. That caused me to start drunkenly yelling at her. I yelled and swore at her. Turning around, having said my piece, I started to walk out of the pub.

A stranger approached me at the bar as I was on the way out. He remonstrated with me over my loud behaviour. It had nothing to do with him and in any event, I was leaving the pub. I told him exactly that but added, 'Fuck off!' I thought that was the end of the matter.

As I was walking out between the two outer doors of the pub, someone grabbed me from behind. My arms were now pinned down by my side. I was furious. I glanced over my shoulder and was able to see it was the same guy who had spoken to me at the bar.

We both staggered out toward a small green outside the pub. He would not let go of me. We both fell and rolled around on the damp grass. It was then I saw the flashing blue lights of several police cars. About ten coppers surrounded us. We were still rolling around on the grass and he still had my arms pinned back.

He shouted, 'I'm a Met Sergeant and I have arrested this man.'

Most of the ten uniformed Surrey police officers who had now arrived started to kick me as I lay on the ground.

Two of them withdrew their batons and started to strike my arms and legs with the heavy stick. I was now even more furious and tried to free myself to fight back. I had no idea this man was an off-duty Metropolitan Police Sergeant. He had never told me that nor showed me any ID.

I was drunk, so drunk that I did not feel any pain. Yet, not so drunk that I failed to recognise a losing battle.

I shouted, 'Okay, okay. I give up,' and stopped struggling. I managed to stand up. My hands were handcuffed behind my back. Some of the uniformed officers led me to a police car, opened the back door and roughly started to push me in there. I spotted the face of a big, ugly cop who had struck me with the baton. Before I eased myself onto the back seat, I headbutted him and watched his nose split wide open. I felt better!

That episode was costly. I was fined £300, a large sum of money in 1981. I also lost my reputation as I now had a real criminal record as opposed to my fake one when undercover. I had been determined to fight to clear my name before a jury. That plan was scuppered when the police craftily lowered the charges from causing actual bodily harm. They reduced them to a simple assault on a police officer. The result of that was that any trial could only be held before a local magistrates' court with no jury.

The initial lesser charges consisted of assaulting nine officers including a female cop. I did not strike a woman at any time. These new charges deprived me of the right to

## THIRTY

a jury trial. Any trial would happen in a local magistrates' court. I knew from experience that these magistrates, local lay businesspeople with no legal training, will believe police witnesses. I reluctantly agreed to plead guilty to six out of the nine charges, but not the one accusing me of striking the woman. The police prosecutor agreed to that.

It was an unpleasant experience from start to finish. I felt humiliated by having my fingerprints and photograph taken. I was more humiliated by being forced to piss on the cell floor. There was no toilet facility and I was refused permission to use a WC when I asked to do so. I have no idea why some police officers are arseholes. I have always tried to live by the creed, 'do unto others as what you would have them do unto you.'

There was now an urgent need to earn money to pay off this huge fine. I drifted about. Sales and selling were better than living on handouts. The "black dog" was never far away and visited me on many occasions. It had a paralysing effect whenever it struck.

I was even tempted to join in a crazy plan to execute a coup on an island off the coast of East Africa. Some ex-military men approached me. They included former SAS members. They thought my police knowledge would be useful when they captured the island's communications centre. I discovered that there was a real chance of live ammunition being fired so I gracefully backed out of the plan. It happened without me some months later.

The passing years saw a continuance of heavy drinking but now it took the form of binge drinking. My career in sales and sales management ended in Britain's severe economic slump between 1989–90.

Once more without work, I gained my HGV licence and could now drive trucks. I did this for about two years and used it to recharge my batteries. It was then I decided to try a career in law. First, I gained a law honours degree at university. Then I passed the Bar exam in London. That postgraduate qualification saw me qualify as a barrister in 1997. I practised criminal law from London chambers until 2011.

Studying for the Bar was tough. I started to smoke cannabis on a regular basis to de-stress. Many barristers in London use cocaine as their recreational drug of choice. I was reacquainted with it during my time as a London barrister. It was nothing like the cocaine Smiles supplied, which I loved. The stuff I was using then induced a severe case of paranoia in me one night. I have never used it since and have no intention of doing so again. I ceased smoking cannabis some years ago after I realised that it was a habit I did not need. My current drinking? Two small bottles of cold beer every night.

I practised as a barrister from chambers in Middle Temple, London, where many *Rumpole of the Bailey* scenes were filmed. I was walking away from the building one day when I saw a familiar face. It was Kevin Dooley, who was by then a successful Liverpool lawyer with his own thriving firm.

I walked on by thinking it looked like him, but he looked too old. Then I remembered that I too was getting older.

'Kevin!'

He stopped in his tracks and we caught up. What he was up to and vice versa.

Kevin had been a young solicitor's clerk at a firm of solicitors based in Kirkby, Merseyside, when I first met him. I was a young rookie jack at Kirkby at the time.

Following up on our chance encounter in London, I travelled to Kirkby to meet him in his office. This was pre-arranged as he told me he could help me.

He regaled me with stories of how he did a lot of legal work for the Merseyside Police Federation. Then he made me a promise to take up my case. His argument was that I had resigned from the police force while suffering from severe depression, a form of mental illness. He told me it was possible that I had a viable case to sue the Hampshire force to claim damages for personal injury because the force had not discharged its duty of care toward me. The major hurdle was the three years' time limit to bring claims of that kind. Kevin accepted that I genuinely had not realised that I was suffering from a medical incapacity until many years after the event.

He filled me with some hope.

I heard nothing more from Kevin.

# THIRTY-ONE

# UNFINISHED BUSINESS

Operation Julie would never have happened but for a man called Gerry Thomas. It was Thomas who ratted on Solomon, Kemp, et al, after his arrest in Canada. He did it in the hope of receiving a lenient sentence. He was facing a life sentence under Canadian law in 1972 for importing 13 pounds. of cannabis into Montreal. His deal saw him serve seven months of a 15-month sentence. He was deported to the USA on his release. Dick Lee eventually caught up with Thomas in Texas in 1976.

Thomas was relieved to see an English police inspector at his door. He confessed to Lee he had been expecting a bullet for informing on the British LSD manufacturing operation. So much for the love and peace espoused by the likes of Kemp. Thomas first met David Solomon and Paul Arnaboldi at Millbrook, New York. All three had been drawn in by the Timothy Leary acid inspired mantra of 'tune in, turn on, drop out'.

Thomas became reacquainted with Solomon in England in 1972. That is when he also met Richard Kemp and Christine Bott. It was now that Solomon bought ergotamine tartrate for Kemp's use in manufacturing LSD. It was

Thomas who also revealed to Lee that it was Andy Munro, later to become Todd's LSD chemist, who was used by Kemp to test the purity of the acid tabs. Kemp suspected Todd was diluting the content before tabletting. Todd, or George, as some knew him, was responsible for tabletting and distribution of Kemp's acid at that time.

Thomas told Lee he believed it was Solomon who had informed on him leading to his arrest in Montreal. There had been a disagreement between the two men. Thomas became angry so he threatened to expose Solomon and Kemp to the British authorities. Solomon, in turn, threatened Thomas with dire consequences if he was foolish enough to do so. So, what would those dire consequences have been? Maybe one needs to look no further than the words uttered by Kemp following his arrest when Kemp realised that all his cash had been seized in the wake of his arrest.

It was Dick Lee and Peter Spencer, one of the Operation Julie detectives, who spoke with Kemp about his Swiss bank safety deposit boxes. Kemp became distraught at the thought of becoming penniless and losing his cottage at Blaencaron, Wales.

He blurted out, 'He's dead.'

Pressed by Dick Lee, Kemp added, 'The slimy bastard over there. Thomas.'

Lee reported that he was taken aback by the hatred and viciousness of Kemp's tone.

Not content with his previous outburst, Kemp also said, 'He's the guy who's put us all here … We knew it would happen and we should have done it years ago. David [Solomon] said he would talk. It doesn't matter, He is dead ... the word has gone out.'

Dick Lee learned that a contract for $10,000 was placed on the head of Thomas.

That apparent conspiracy to murder Thomas should have been thoroughly investigated and parties to the crime arrested and prosecuted. Who better equipped to conduct that investigation than the existing Operation Julie team? We were detectives first and foremost. There was no sound reason to limit our sphere of investigations solely to drugs and LSD.

Prior to writing this book, I discovered Operation Julie had a further link to terrorists. David Solomon, for me, was always a dark character. I always felt there was something sinister about him. He was the man who had the links to the Brotherhood of Eternal Love. He had approached Kemp to manufacture both LSD and a synthesised form of cannabis. It turns out he also associated with IRA terrorists. He also had links to other terrorists. These links were never followed up. The individual chief officers of police, no doubt backed up by the Home Office, were satisfied that Operation Julie had run its full course. It had fulfilled its remit of identifying the people behind the manufacturing of the LSD and the associated distribution network. It was a short-sighted decision and akin to turning a blind eye to other serious criminals and terrorists.

Prior to finishing this book, someone contacted me with information connecting Solomon to known terrorists. He was adamant that Solomon did have connections to the IRA. I queried this with him out of curiosity and some scepticism. He responded with more information.

It appears that Solomon, Kemp, and Bott paid my correspondent's father a visit. They were keen to buy a property in Anglesey, Wales, no doubt as a front to manufacture LSD. The deal didn't go through. Solomon wrote to the father expressing regret at the non-completion of the deal.

He emailed me a copy of a letter written by Solomon and sent it to his father. It's interesting as it is dated 1972 and shows Solomon's address as Randolph Avenue, London, W9. It was an address we were aware of during the investigation. It is even more interesting when Solomon refers to his 'clan'. To me, it is indicative that he perceived himself as a leader or father figure of the British group.

My correspondent went on to explain why he thought I was wrong to exculpate IRA involvement in the Operation Julie drugs conspiracy. I had made a throwaway remark to that effect when I wrote a pre-publication blog post about this book. He distinctly recalls an IRA volunteer named as James McCann visiting his father in the company of Solomon. A 'volunteer' was a name given to a Provisional IRA terrorist.

It was believed that some Provos, as they were known, were involved in drug running, weapons smuggling and racketeering to provide a war fund to fight the British. The drugs trade was a lucrative source of income. Some sources claim that the IRA was anti drugs. That may have been the case among the older, wiser figures. But McCann did not fit into either of those categories. The correspondent described seeing McCann 'going mental' at his father. To this day, the son doesn't know why. Solomon calmed the Irishman down and they left.

Sadly, the writer told me that his father died regretting that the Operation Julie investigation had not tied up the loose ends and followed up on this IRA link. It was unfinished business as far as his father was concerned.

McCann was by all accounts a volatile character and so it was no surprise that my correspondent, then a young boy, witnessed the Provo 'going mental' at his father.

Of course, these loose ends were a by-product of the establishment, forcing an end to Dick Lee and the Operation Julie investigation. If we had been permitted to really dig deep, who knows what we may have discovered?

During the investigation, there were unsubstantiated links, allegations and rumours concerning Princess Margaret, Mossad and the CIA. Perhaps therein lies the real reason the establishment stopped us from pursuing unfinished business? There again, if allowed to continue, we may have found ourselves in a different league!

A man called Ronald Stark was of great interest to us. There was a link between Stark and McCann. So what do we know about people like McCann and Stark? Tendler and

May[14] describe how James McCann, at the time a rising star in the Provisional IRA, firebombed a Belfast university. He was arrested along with two American journalists. The journalists were released owing to Ronald Stark's intervention. Stark also took an interest in McCann. That interest led to the security services taking an interest in Stark. Dick Lee found that out when trying to track down Stark during the early days of Operation Julie. He found that MI5 had already had Stark in their sights.

McCann fled Belfast and set up as a cannabis dealer in Amsterdam. Stark is a shadowy mystery figure. He was known to the DEA in 1972. It has been said that the files at that time only showed what Stark was not, not what he was. Stark surfaced later when he was arrested in connection with a find of over 33lbs of hash in Holland. He had claimed to be a Lebanese bound for New York. He was again arrested on arrival in the United States on a passport violation. DEA agents began to reconstruct an earlier San Francisco LSD case against him. They found it impossible to do so after such a long time and Stark was released.

One thing is clear, Stark was a successful LSD entrepreneur and appeared to be wealthy. He was known to be involved with a man named Druce. He was a British man, who dealt in ergotamine tartrate (the base ingredient for the manufacture of LSD) as a commodity broker. Druce came to the attention of Operation Julie but was never charged as at that time dealing in ergotamine tartrate was perfectly legal. Sources show that Stark was producing LSD in Rome in the 1960s. It is also known that he moved to France, running LSD manufacturing fronted by legitimate chemical companies in Paris. It was here, around 1969 in one version, that he employed Kemp as a chemist in the manufacture of LSD. Following his arrest in Operation Julie, Kemp admitted to being a passenger in Stark's Ferrari in 1970. That is when it was checked by British Customs at Dover.

Tendler and May[15] reported that 'any cursory study of Stark would reveal that he appears to have stepped from rags to riches'. He had expensive luxury cars and a house in Greenwich Village, Manhattan. He spoke many languages and travelled the world. In 1969, he met an American expatriate in Paris who mentioned Solomon to Stark. David Solomon's roots went back to the Brotherhood of Eternal Love's Millbrook days. It was through David Solomon that Stark met Kemp.

Richard Kemp always maintained that he had nothing to do with the Brotherhood of Eternal Love, yet reliable sources of information contradicted that denial. It was believed that senior figures in the Brotherhood had visited Kemp and Stark in Paris in 1970. They ordered them to shut down production owing to US Federal law enforcement paying close attention to the Brotherhood in California. Furthermore, Kemp, by his own admission, met Nick Sand and Lester Friedman, both senior members of the Brotherhood, in Switzerland in 1970. It beggars belief that

Kemp, an educated intelligent man, would not know that he was dealing with the Brotherhood. He produced a huge batch of LSD in Paris for Stark that was destined to be sold in America. Or was there an alternative explanation behind Kemp distancing himself from the Brotherhood? Was Kemp the UK subsidiary of the Brotherhood of Love, Inc.?

This alternative scenario was one we should have been permitted to investigate. Could it have been that Kemp's British LSD manufacturing was part of the Brotherhood's plan? Did the Brotherhood possess the foresight that the American authorities were closing in on them? In 1972, the Americans shut down the Brotherhood's USA West Coast laboratories. It was the same year that Thomas was arrested in Canada and Timothy Leary in Afghanistan. By then, Kemp was in full-swing manufacturing his acid in Britain.

Dick Lee, using the services of Interpol, traced Stark to Rome in the early stages of Operation Julie. He was in prison serving a 14-year sentence for drugs importation. He had been arrested in 1975 in Bologna. He was carrying a false passport and in possession of large quantities of cannabis, morphine and cocaine. Lee discovered the existence of Starks's Rome safety-deposit box. It contained papers detailing the process of manufacturing LSD. It was exactly the same process used by Kemp.

Stark saw the opportunity for marketing the French, Kemp-manufactured acid in the United States. The business opportunity took the form of the Brotherhood of Eternal

Love. Stark travelled to California to meet the Brothers. Stark fascinated the Brothers and impressed them. At that time, were afraid of losing their ranch as a result of police raids. Stark had answers, and said he had access to lawyers who could fix such problems. Tendler and May, in their book, had this to say:

> As for LSD, Sand was still tabletting but had no immediate prospects of a laboratory without raw materials. In return for a feedback of money and materials, Stark could fill the gap. The LSD would be made in Europe, in a laboratory safely out of reach of the American authorities, and dyed orange to continue the flow of Orange Sunshine. To spice the offer, Stark added that he had discovered a new quick process of making LSD and even had the assistance of an English chemist who, he claimed, had done research for a Nobel Prize-winning team.

There are no prizes for guessing that Stark was talking about Richard Kemp. Those same authors added:

> Ronald Stark was and is an enigma. Many people can describe him and remember conversations or events, yet they cannot say who exactly he really was. With a clutch of different identities, he moved like a chameleon from communes and LSD laboratories to luxury hotels and exclusive gentlemen's clubs. The major LSD producer who

*became adviser and partner of the pacific Brothers was also adviser and confidant of terrorists, walking with Arab princes and Sicilian Mafiosi. He was the man who made LSD a transatlantic commodity, the catalyst for a British subsidiary which became one of the world's greatest LSD producers.*

*If Owsley was, according to Leary, God's Secret Agent, for whom did Stark work? There is no one word which accurately describes Stark ... and that is the way he wanted it. Stark operated on four continents, in at least a dozen countries. He did so for the most part successfully because in the Americas they knew little about what he did in Europe, just as those in Europe knew very little about what he had done in Africa, and those in Africa knew nothing about his activities in Asia. His textbook for security, exhorting others to follow his example, was, of all things, a science-fiction novel published in the 1960s by Robert A. Heinlein, called The Moon Is A Harsh Mistress. It is the story of a lunar colony's attempt to free itself from the control of Earth through a movement based on a system of cells, each kept in ignorance of the others. The success of the revolution is also aided by skilful deployment of disinformation.*

*In this, Stark was a past master. There is not one biography but two, three, four or more different stories which he disseminated. Each is slightly different, so that no two people ever got the same story.*

Clearly Stark was worthy of investigation by the Operation Julie team. He was never interviewed by us. Dick Lee sought permission to go to the Rome prison where Stark was serving his sentence to interview him. He got short shrift – that was beyond the remit of Operation Julie!

Another piece of unfinished business was the Israeli Izchak Sheni. He was known as Zani to us on the Operation Julie team as that was how he was known to Mark Tcharney and Solomon. Zani was a dealer in heroin and LSD based in Amsterdam. He supplied drugs to Israel and other countries worldwide. One source of information was adamant that he also supplied LSD to Mossad, the Israeli secret police.

The informant added that Mossad, in turn, supplied the CIA with some of this LSD. Solomon used Tcharney as a courier to deliver the Kemp acid to Zani in Amsterdam. The remit for Operation Julie was to bring the manufacturers and the distribution network to justice. Zani was a key player in that distribution network. At one stage of the investigation Dick Lee was as excited about this dealer as any other, if not more so. For some reason that excitement waned, and Zani seemed to become a forgotten link. My own thoughts on that? Lee was warned off by the security services either in Britain or overseas.

Paul Joseph Arnaboldi escaped justice for his major role in helping Kemp manufacture LSD at Carno, mid-Wales. He procured and supplied the ergotamine tartrate; purchased Plas Llysin; and according to Kemp left Carno with five-pounds weight of pure LSD crystal. Something he bragged about to friends in Belize.

That, too, is unfinished business and is partly explained because, following the disbandment of the Operation Julie squad, no detective or police force bothered to track him down. He remains a man of mystery and, according to some, was known by the name of 'The Crow' to cover his international drug dealing. I now know he lived openly in Deià, Majorca, for many years before buying a castle in northern Spain.

After it became possible to extradite fugitives from Spain to the United Kingdom, he relocated and bought houses in the Dominican Republic, Belize and Mexico, and lived a free life in all those countries until he died in 2020, aged 92 years, in Patzcuaro, Mexico. He had been living under the alias of Juan Banes Lopez, but known as 'Josh' to many of his expatriate friends and paid infrequent visits to the United States where his brother, a successful tax lawyer, lived.

I call him a man of mystery as no one seems to know exactly what he was doing between 1976 and his death. The stories and rumours continue abound, not least in Majorca. Most people who knew him in those days seem to fall into two camps. They either despised him or were fond of him. The former based their feelings on the shabby way he treated women, particularly younger women. The tale of his having undergone cosmetic facial surgery in Thailand is repeated by several of the people who knew him. It seems he confided in many that he did this to reduce the chances of his arrest following Operation Julie.

# THIRTY-TWO

# LESSONS LEARNED

Many lessons should have been learned from Operation Julie. I have no idea if they were. If they were, I do not know if they were acted upon. These are my thoughts on what was learned and what should have become standard practice.

Undercover operatives, or UCs as the Americans call them, surveillance teams and telephone intercepts are the golden formulae for combatting organised crime gangs. They have limited use in isolation from each other. They must overlap and dovetail with each other for maximum effect.

Let me give you a classic example from Operation Julie. In the hot summer of 1976, Martyn Pritchard had become cosy with Lochhead and McDonnell, the two Wiltshire-based dealers. He was undercover and accepted by those two dealers. They were an easy touch compared to the ultra-cautious Smiles. The telephone tap commenced after Pritchard had snuggled up to them. It soon became apparent that they were dealing in LSD and other drugs to the tune of £10,000 per month. What's more, the tap revealed that their major source of supply was a woman called Monica and a man in Wales, David John Robertson. Nothing was known of Monica save for her first name and place of work in London.

Lee sent a surveillance team to London. They successfully located Monica. The team followed her to a basement flat in Camden Town, north London. She was kept under surveillance for some time and was later confirmed as Monica Kenyon. It became clear she was living with a man called Tony and was assisting him in the distribution of drugs. At this stage, Tony had not been identified.

Pritchard arranged for a test purchase of LSD from the two Wiltshire suppliers. Sure enough, after he had ordered a sample of 500 tabs, Lochhead and McDonnell were heard talking to Monica on the phone tap and discussing the order. The surveillance team then saw Monica enter the basement flat. Tony left the flat and walked over to a public telephone kiosk across the street. He was heard accepting the order (a price of £145) and arranging the handover later that day on the M4 Motorway.

The two Wiltshire dealers returned from the handover and gave the acid tabs to Pritchard in exchange for £160. A few days later, Lochhead was heard trying to contact Monica for a further order of LSD but without success. She had gone away for a few days with Tony. Undeterred, Lochhead also tried Robertson, another supplier, but again without any luck.

In desperation, he dialled a new number …

LOCHHEAD: This is Stuart. I can't get hold of Tony or Dave at Brecon.

DEALER: Man, what the hell are you doing? Ringing me?

LOCHHEAD: I want some urgently and thought it would be alright to ring you.

DEALER: You cunt! You know you don't ring me.

LOCHHEAD: Yeah, I'm sorry man. But can you help me?

DEALER: Okay, how many?

LOCHHEAD: Three, please.

DEALER: Jesus, only three? It's not worth my time!

LOCHHEAD: I'll come and collect them.

DEALER: Don't bother. I'll post them to Tony. You get them from him. And never ring this number again.

Back in Devizes, Dave Redrup believed he knew the person behind the number dialled by Lochhead. He checked and confirmed it was the home number of Smiles at Y Glyn. In turn, an application was made for a tap on that line. He was a bigger fish. He thought a request for 3,000 tabs of acid was small fry.

Although Eric and I were then in situ in Llanddewi Brefi, Smiles was way too cautious to allow us to do a Pritchard and Lochhead/McDonnell number. But the fact we were in place was still important for us to gather intelligence on Smiles. It was clear that he was dealing in tens of thousands of acid tabs. And that Tony (later identified as Tony Dalton) and Monica were part of his London connections. Monica Kenyon, carelessly referred to by Buzz as Mon in our presence one day in the New Inn.

The value of the unholy trinity of undercover, surveillance and telephone taps working in perfect harmony is amply demonstrated by that episode. No matter whether it be drugs, thieves, racketeers or terrorists, that approach can be applied to any criminal organisation. Of course, each limb of the trinity has its own uses in isolation. For example, Eric and I uncovered the plot to import vast quantities of cocaine into Britain without the aid of surveillance or telephone taps.

• • •

The other lessons learned are personal. Firstly, a potential undercover infiltrator must be willing to subject themselves to rigorous psychological testing before embarking on their role. The appropriate professionals must deem that person as fit for purpose. It is a first step in the duty of care that is owed to officers involved in such potentially dangerous and stressful work.

If deemed fit, there should be a training programme of sorts. Ideally, it should be run by veterans. My experience has been completely lost to the police service when it could have been valuable to younger officers. It is not possible to teach everything involved in undercover work but as a minimum, rookie undercover operatives should be prepared for as many eventualities as possible.

This type of work is unique. It deserves recognition with a different pay structure than regular officers. Of course, I mean an enhanced pay scale. It should be a career path of its own within the police service. There is no reason why a competent undercover officer should be compelled to return to normality and normal duties on completion of an assignment. They can be given a break and return to a new undercover assignment another day in another location. They can return under a new identity if called for. Good undercover people don't grow on trees. It is a special ability. They deserve to be taken care of financially, physically and mentally. Safeguards can be put in place to avoid burnout or mental health problems.

There is another feature of undercover work I rarely see discussed. It is a feature that needs rigorous safeguards built into the supervision of undercover officers. There is sometimes a temptation to join forces with the other side, to switch teams. During my time with Bill and Blue, I did give thought to the easy riches associated with major drug trafficking. There was a temptation to go solo. As a deep undercover operative, you are by definition a risk-taker. It is only a short step to becoming involved as a player. These were not idle thoughts. I did consider the attractions and fringe benefits. What stopped me? Integrity, professional pride and the thought of doing serious time if caught.

Law enforcement in Britain needs to think out of the box when considering the recruitment and deployment of undercover officers. Why recruit for such roles within the police service? There is a case to be made for a secret all-agency national undercover force. Suitable recruits need not be police officers. They are suitable because of their abilities and personalities, not because they once wore a uniform.

Such a pool of expert UCs could be deployed in many situations. The individual UC may be used for infiltrating drugs gangs, organised crime gangs and terrorist groups. An individual would be selected for a particular task according to his or her ethnicity. There is not much advantage to placing a UC with a British-Asian background into a white supremacy gang. Likewise, there is no mileage in asking a white female UC to infiltrate an Islamic-fundamentalist terror organisation.

Finally, the stress of the role, if to be a career lifestyle, should warrant an early retirement package with attractive pension benefits. Never again should chief officers of the police or any police supervisor allow an undercover officer to resign when on sick leave, particularly when that sickness is a mental health problem caused by the undercover work.

Am I angry? Am I bitter? After all these years? Most of the time the anger and bitterness were buried below the surface. In writing this memoir I have been forced to relive memories and face up to the facts. Let me put it this way – I now passionately believe I was treated shabbily by the police service. It's not that I regret the life I have lived since resigning from the police force. I believe I became a better, more rounded person. The writing has been cathartic. I have tried to be frank in every detail. Even my good friend, Eric, after reading a draft manuscript, thought I was doing a self-assassination job. I know what he meant, and I value his opinion. But Eric, I am imperfect. I have character traits that even you knew nothing about until you read my manuscript.

These truths I write about are why I have started and stopped this book countless times. I was not prepared to be brutally honest with myself until recently. I wasn't capable of that. Maybe I am being harsh on myself? Maybe the picture I have painted is not the complete picture. I don't know. That is for others who know me well to decide.

Those who know me well are entitled to form an opinion about me and my undercover role. I confess I have had some difficulty with strangers who chose to leave vile, anonymous remarks about me following promotional articles about my undercover days published in various magazines. I guess it is a feature of this digital age. I have toned down my original reaction to these ill-informed vicious comments.

I do believe that people like that must be out of touch with reality. They remind me of people I knew when I was a young detective. People who professed to hate all cops. But what happened to them when they or their close family were the victims of a serious crime? They became transformed overnight. They would cooperate with the police and act courteously. Above all, they would appreciate that the police have a difficult job.

I accept opinions on undercover tactics, and I mean legitimate tactics, will vary. It remains a source of comfort to me to know that all the people who have mattered in my life admired me for my undercover exploits. That extends to most total strangers, too. My undercover peers hold me in good regard. Indeed, one of them, a Vietnam veteran and former undercover US Customs Special Agent, told me he could not have done what I did. I was astounded knowing he had made buys from Colombian cartels with show money of $200,000! As for my thoughts? I always return to the question in the title of Chapter One – *Who am I?* My battles are personal. They remain in my head.

Is such an elite squad ever likely to happen? I doubt it especially now the UK government is involved in determining the future of undercover policing.

### Future of Undercover Policing

Twitter is awash with the #spycops hashtag. It is an omen of things to come relating to the UK's UCPI – Undercover Policing Inquiry[16], now chaired by Sir John Mitting, a former High Court judge who replaced Lord Justice Pitchford following his resignation due to ill health.

The Inquiry was set up in the wake of several scandals involving undercover police tactics. Those are well documented elsewhere, but what I hope that the Inquiry asks, 'Is there such a thing as ethical undercover policing?' To some that appears to be an oxymoron. Perhaps it comes as no surprise when learning about some of the antics of former Metropolitan Police Service (MPS) undercover officers.

There are occasions when undercover tactics go too far. Two such events that I have in mind are the 'Lizzie' and Colin Stagg affair, and the relationships scandal involving Mark Kennedy.

Let me make it clear – I do not condone any of the actions of those officers and former officers. What they did was beyond the pale. I just cannot accept that living with a woman in a relationship for some length of time with the intention of cementing a "back story" or "legend" is okay by any standards. It got even worse when one officer fathered a child because of the duplicitous relationship. I am referring to the case of Mark Kennedy, an undercover officer who fathered a child in furtherance of the maintenance of his cover. Owing to his despicable antics, and those of other undercover officers, it became necessary for the government to establish the Undercover Policing Inquiry.

In the Colin Stagg case, Lizzie was an undercover officer designated to befriend Colin Stagg. who was suspected (and later completely exonerated) of the murder of Rachel Nickell on Wimbledon Common in 1992. A criminal psychologist, a profiler, and the police had decided that Stagg matched the criteria. A profiler was subsequently requested to assist in designing a covert operation to see whether Stagg would eliminate or implicate himself through his friendship with 'Lizzie'. This operation was later severely criticised by the media and Stagg's trial judge as a honey trap. When the case reached the Old Bailey, Mr Justice Ognall ruled that the police had shown 'excessive zeal' and had tried to incriminate a suspect by 'deceptive conduct of the grossest kind'. He excluded the entrapment evidence and the prosecution withdrew its case. Stagg was formally acquitted in September 1994.

During their interactions, Stagg was deliberately led by 'Lizzie' into discussions about the violent sexual fantasies. She feigned a predilection for these types of fantasy. This went too far. Her supervisors ought to have known better and she should have refused to be a party to the nonsense.

There was misguided supervision in Lizzie's case and it appears there was a total lack of effective supervision in the Mark Kennedy case.

There is something about the MPS. It always had the reputation of being a law to itself back in my day. Tales of corruption were rife and unsurprisingly often proven to be true. The Met looked down upon their 'country cousins' no matter they also may have happened to copper in a large city. The Met always believed they were superior. Of course, this irked us provincial coppers and we had good reason to distrust them. It is a pity. Many Met officers were and are fine police officers. It's always the case that the few bad apples turn the barrel rotten, to indulge in a little metaphor mangling.

Can undercover policing be ethical? Some may argue it never can because it is duplicitous by its nature. Yes, it is but serious crime is both a burden to and a threat to society. There surely is room for undercover law enforcement activities to thwart serious organised crime? I believe so and those tactics must be reserved for the most serious of crimes – terrorism, major drug trafficking, people trafficking, etc. It should never again be used for infiltrating protest groups or political organisations with one caveat – unless those groups are engaging in serious crime. Peaceful protest and political affiliation are neither crimes nor warrant undercover tactics or police intrusion.

It is also clear that the ability to conduct covert undercover operations must be taken away from local commanders. The UK in recent times has seen a proliferation in undercover drugs 'buy and bust' operations. It's a wonder these undercover 'narcos' didn't end up arresting each other as every nick in every force seemed to be running such tactics. Furthermore, it also led to a practice of undercover officers urging street-level dealers to big it up – increasing from their usual weight of an eighth to supplying a kilo of the product. That is wrong and, in all probability, is also entrapment and thus unlawful.

Those kinds of operations were born out of a need to make the figures look good. Statistics have always been the bane of policing and good policing ought not to be concentrated on shuffling paperwork and submitting statistics. Thwarting serious crime has nothing to do with collating statistics. Combating organised crime is intelligence-driven. Sadly, like many other areas of life, the police service has become a politically correct organisation. It is driven by men and women of officer rank who have never experienced the day-to-day fight against serious crime. How do I know that? I point you in the direction of the recent undercover 'rule book' published by the College of Policing[17].

It is a document riddled with jargon and not without some ridiculous notions. It was clearly drafted by people who have never partaken in deep undercover work. My success as a deep undercover officer was partially owed to my using drugs on a regular basis. Now under the current regime's proposals, I would be subjecting myself to both criminal and disciplinary proceedings.

Possibly the most laughable idea floated in that document is the urging of undercover operatives to adhere to the Working Time Directive[18]. Perhaps I have missed something, but I fail to see a connection with lorry drivers and undercover cops.

Undercover policing is a valuable tool in the fight against serious crime. I hope the Inquiry doesn't result in the baby being thrown out with the bathwater. I have confidence in the Inquiry but none whatsoever in the leadership and direction of the modern British police service.

This chapter is titled 'Lessons Learned.' One of the greatest lessons learned is that in retrospect Operation Julie was a waste of time. It led directly or indirectly to fine detectives lost to the police force. The efforts and skills were never utilised in the fight against real criminals. Julie was not the start of the 'war on drugs'. It was just the wrong war.

Whichever way I look at it I still can't get over a feeling that I betrayed a good friend. Damn it, Smiles!

Why were you so likeable?

## THIRTY-THREE

# DUPLICITY

Working undercover is duplicitous. Duplicity goes together with being an undercover cop. Think of bacon and eggs, toast and jam – I think you get the idea. Duplicity plays a part in many everyday situations. It is practised every day by countless people worldwide such as unfaithful spouses, politicians and unscrupulous businesspeople. Duplicity is, unfortunately, an integral part of the human condition. I ask, considering my experiences, is there an acceptable form of duplicity even within the context of law enforcement?

To behave in a duplicitous fashion is to act in a two-faced manner. In an everyday setting, it is unacceptable. We have all known people who speak out as if agreeing with different people. The trouble is that the duplicitous person will agree with a different opinion to suit his or her own ends.

Politics is the classic setting for acts of duplicity. Politicians will say one thing to one person for a vote or support. At the same time, he or she will tell the opposition exactly what they want to hear even if it is the polar opposite of a previous position. This goes on in the lobby rooms and corridors of power all the time. The deceitful politician must know he will be found out but does not care.

Duplicity is not confined to politics. It occurs in business, as well. Some salespeople will tell potential customers anything to get a sale. It may even be a lie about costs or safety factors of a product. There have been scandals in the motor industry, for instance, in which it appears that insiders fully aware of the safety hazards on certain cars chose to lie to the company, and to the public.

One of the intriguing things about duplicity is the actor's belief that it will never be uncovered. Yet in this age of the internet and instant news, a newsworthy story about duplicity can be shared millions of times over in the time it takes to boil a kettle.

Duplicity becomes an art form when applied to police undercover work or espionage. Duplicity is not the preserve of the good guys, the agents on the side of law enforcement who make tremendous sacrifices to keep you and me safe. There are many examples of duplicitous bad guys, too.

Whichever way one looks at duplicity, it is undeniably a form of excitement. As a young man engaged in undercover work, it excited me. I found it different and a challenge.

The duplicity I engaged in during my time undercover is obvious and documented within these pages. What may not be so obvious is just how far the devious mind will go in fostering and perpetuating the lie.

I had every admiration for Dick Lee but he was devious. He would play both parties or all the parties if it suited his ends. An example of this is when Martyn Pritchard was undercover during Operation Julie. Lee frequently mentioned an informant called Swan in his book. Swan offered to reveal some interesting information to Lee about some of the main players in the Operation Julie network. Those players were believed to be involved at the top of the organisation. But Swan made a demand that Lee was uncomfortable with. Swan wanted Lee to fund a drug smuggling operation that Swan would operate and expect total immunity from arrest and prosecution. Lee considered the proposition and was tempted yet he found a solution, a duplicitous solution.

Lee concluded that Swan was mostly concerned about being ripped off by other drug dealers, which was a common occurrence in the drugs world. So he made an alternative proposal to Swan. He would arrange for a heavy to accompany him to any meeting where drugs and cash were to be exchanged. Swan was delighted and gratefully accepted the offer. The heavy in question was Martyn Pritchard. This was a win-win situation for Lee. He got the information Swan had offered. He also got additional drugs information Swan volunteered to Pritchard and he received feedback on the veracity of the information supplied by Swan. It was as if Lee was next to Swan at these times but Swan was not aware of it because Lee, in fact, was Pritchard. Dick Lee was never afraid to take chances. That was one of the reasons I liked him. Often he sailed a little too close to the rocks but like all great generals, or captains if you don't like mixed metaphors, he was lucky.

You, the reader, may have picked up on something I wrote earlier in the book. It was a subtle hint that when I was in Liverpool, I had wondered about Blue's bona fides. For many years, I still pondered on the same thing until lately.

A few years after Operation Julie was all over, I visited Dick Lee in Scarborough, North Yorkshire. As best as I can recall it was about 1986. Dick's wife, Pam, had cooked a pheasant and we had a delicious family lunch together. After lunch was finished, Pam did something that reminded me of bygone days. She started to clear the table and suggested that Dick and I be left alone to talk about men's business.

We chatted naturally enough about Operation Julie and some of the characters involved in it on both sides of the fence. Dick Lee was a convivial host and an intelligent man, yet sometimes he came out with ridiculous thoughts. One such ridiculous thought was about a former colleague. He told me a bullshit story that was beyond belief.

'Oh, away and fuck yourself. That's a joke,' was my response.

He recognised my ire and our conversation turned to normality. Dick Lee loved a good conspiracy theory. I had heard many conspiracy theories in the aftermath of Operation Julie. Stuff like how Julie officers had financially gained from the operation. No doubt people were saying the same sort of thing about me. I heard some weird and wonderful stories about how key members of the squad had discovered hidden hordes of drug money and split it up among themselves. In a similar vein, we had apparently also found thousands of buried LSD tabs and sold them to hungry dealers. All these stories were garbage.

Dick opened another bottle of malt. We had drunk a few more glasses when I caught him off guard.

I queried, 'What about Blue then?'

He gave that wry smile of his. It was a ploy he often used. It didn't mean a thing. I believe people tried to read something into that Lee smirk but they were wasting their time. You see, it was used as a delaying tactic. It gave him time to think of the ramifications of a question or a given situation. Its meaning was everything and nothing.

He replied, 'What do you mean?' as he was still grinning like a Cheshire cat. It could be infuriating but I had gotten to know his quirks.

'What happened to Blue and Bill? You can tell me now. We are both out of the job.'

He straightened his face and said, 'They were both dealt with by the DEA.'

'What does that mean? Dealt with?'

'There was a big sting operation going on over in the States. A massive cocaine and heroin trafficking operation. You and Eric stumbled onto it. They finished it off and your guys are doing 25 years in a federal penitentiary.'

'Hmm.'

'What's that supposed to mean, Bentley?'

'I have a theory.'

Dick laughed, 'I suppose I had better listen then.'

I rolled out my theory. Dick listened closely as I went through my alternative theory in some detail.

Lee said, 'Is that it?'

'Yes.'

He gave that smirk of his once more, saying, 'You are a clever bastard.'

That answer was infuriating because it wasn't an answer. I never got a straight answer from Dick Lee. In any event, and with the passage of time, it turns out my theory was utterly wrong.

One more thing – my duplicity was clear to see during my stint undercover. Did I mean all I have written about Smiles?

You need to turn to the next page for the answer.

## THIRTY-FOUR

# SMILES REVISITED

You bet! He was a great guy. We just had our different roles in life. My life has been a little richer by meeting him. He is one of life's great characters. There aren't many left.

The pointless 'war on drugs' left a scar on both of our lives.

I am informed the relationship between Smiles and I has fascinated many people. That is what prompted this chapter. That relationship has caused me conflict to this day and as one observer put it, 'The longer Bentley remained undercover … the more conflicted he became.'

A BBC journalist commented after reading my book that 'The whole idea of turning into someone else is absolutely fascinating.'

Therein lies the conundrum. Yes, I turned into someone else when I was undercover but both the someone else (Steve Jackson) and the real me liked Smiles.

Someone reminded me of what Smiles *thinks* he said on first meeting Eric and me. 'Have a drink, officers. You're off duty,' Smiles told various people for decades when recalling the day Steve Jackson and Eric Walker walked into the New Inn. It's a good line because it's funny. Funnier still, neither Eric nor I recollect him saying anything like that. I concede that is the kind of thing he might say. It is Smiles's way. His method of operating. He loves to tease. Let's face it, he was living beyond the law and had the art of self-preservation off to a tee.

Smiles earned his living by selling drugs. He was wary of strangers particularly if they showed up at his 'manor' in rural Wales. Any stranger could have been an undercover cop. Jackson was. Over the course of the next eight months after that first encounter, Jackson grew fond of Smiles. So fond of him that he came close to revealing it all. A revelation that would have made him a pariah for life in police circles not to mention the real possibility of endangering the safety of other officers.

Steve Jackson lived with the sense of betraying a close friend for 40 years. It never left him. It was a feeling that became part of the fabric of him. Smiles, on the other hand, had to live with the ever-present question, both while serving his eight-year prison term and after.

That question posed to him was probably along these lines:

'You must have known they were cops, right?'

'I knew straight away. I was never fooled,' came the gist of the response.

A face-saving exercise both within and without prison walls. A response that is probably so well rehearsed that Smiles himself believes in its veracity.

Jackson (and Bentley) would point to many things to undermine Smiles's assertion:

- Why would Smiles have asked Jackson to supply serious quantities of cocaine after learning what had happened in Liverpool with the Canadian gangster?
- Why didn't Smiles warn anyone in the drug distribution network? Clearly, he didn't as the telephone intercepts would surely have disclosed the warning.
- Why didn't that intercept record any suspicions he harboured about Jackson and his friend, Walker?
- The LSD manufacturing run at Seymour Road continued as normal, as did the activities of all the drug dealers involved in supplying about 90 per cent of the world's LSD at that time.
- Why did he leave Walker alone babysitting in his home on the night of the cocaine-fuelled night out with Jackson and others in Lampeter?
- Why did he supply Jackson with cannabis and cocaine? Why give Jackson a Christmas gift of cannabis?
- Why were Jackson and Walker frequent welcome and invited guests in his home?
- Why did Smiles choose to be a regular heavy session drinking buddy of Jackson?
- Why was Smiles content to leave a drunken Doug with only Jackson and Walker for company after a drinking session in Tregaron? After all, Doug was one of Smiles's London dealers.
- Why did he often talk about drug dealing with Jackson?
- Why has he made claims that he was told of Jackson's identity and yet did nothing about it?

Falling back on my other occupation of barrister (trial counsel) and contrary to popular belief, a barrister never utters the words, 'I rest my case.' It is far more likely that any barrister in a criminal trial would use the following phrase in addressing the jury, 'You may think, members of the jury ...'

You may think all Smiles's claims are nonsense. I know they are.

That view is reinforced by Llyn Ebenezer, who at the time was a local journalist. He is quoted in a BBC News article[19] as saying:

> *But we didn't have a clue what was going on with these strange groups who'd moved in.*
>
> *To be honest, if anyone seemed more likely to be drug dealers then it was the police acting as hippies, as the actual dealers were all educated professional people who stood their round and blended in really well into the community.*
>
> *The dealers and the police would all be drinking in the pub together, getting up to all sorts of daft capers, so when the raids finally came we all had one hell of a shock.*

None of this takes away Jackson's sense of guilt. This was a friend and in many ways the relationship between Jackson and Smiles became a bromance. There was a genuine bond between them and a sense of ease in each other's company. Steve Jackson felt closer to Smiles than his undercover partner. I don't say that lightly.

# THIRTY-FOUR

On learning that Smiles's great buddy Buzz had died, I passed on my condolences and genuine sympathy to Smiles through social media.

Even now the confusion reigns in my own mind. Where do Steve Bentley and Steve Jackson separate? Are they two people or one?

It seems to me the warmth I once had, still have to a lesser degree, is not reciprocated. Perhaps it's a measure of my feelings towards the man that I felt rebuffed when I read his last message to me. It was petty.

I know I was instrumental in his downfall but he knew the 'rules.' I remain genuinely sorry for being partly responsible for shattering his cosy world, his empire, his family life.

It appears that his "no hard feelings" spoken to me in a police cell in 1977 has dissipated to a degree. So be it. It has helped me put the episode into the annals of my personal history.

Or to take an alternative view, has Steve Bentley put these events of long ago behind him? Is it the case Steve Jackson still has fond memories and yearns for the old days in his old age?

Is it a mix of the two? Perhaps.

## THIRTY-FIVE

# WHERE ARE THEY NOW?

Many have wondered about where all these characters who played a part in Operation Julie have got to. The same applies to those Eric and I mixed with at that time when we were undercover who were not indicted as one of the conspirators. Where are they? What are they doing now?

As for Smiles, he recently died at home surrounded by his wife and family. His great pal, Buzz, died a few years before Smiles. At Buzz's funeral, I am reliably informed he was on great form and gave away some 'free product,' whatever that may have been!

Blue contacted me through social media. He is as friendly as ever and lives in an idyllic spot somewhere in rural England. He denies nothing about his interactions with me and recognises he has lived a life blessed with the luck of the Irish.

### The Others

Richard Kemp has broken his self-imposed exile and now lives in a remote part of Spain. 'Leaf' Fielding, and David Solomon are dead, as is Christine Bott and so is Paul Joseph Arnaboldi as I wrote earlier.

As for my former Operation Julie colleagues, I am still in touch with several of them. Eric and I have never lost touch. I was saddened to hear of Mike Clifford's death recently. Dick Lee died in a hospice in his native Scarborough in August 2016. RIP Guvnor! You were one great operational boss.

Dennis Greenslade also passed away recently. Sadly, I also learned Richie Parry and Noir Bowen have passed away. Martyn Pritchard died some years back, as did his undercover partner, Andy Beaumont. I have also learned that Pauline Tilley died after a long illness.

There are also others that form a backdrop to the Operation Julie saga. Those who were affected in one way or another. For example, the former wife of 'Happy' who got in touch to leave me a pleasant message. Jeff also passed on a goodwill message through a third party. He was the artist Eric and I took to Kent to deliver his painting.

As for me? I write.

Operation Julie appears destined to never go away. It is part of the British fabric, a part of the history of British popular culture. It's as if it was an icon of the drug-influenced 1970s. The year 2018, ushered in the fortieth anniversary of the sentencing of the conspirators. My bet is that you will continue to hear and see quite a lot about Operation Julie.

# AFTERWORD

There cannot be any serious doubt Operation Julie is a part of the fabric of British social history, judging by the mass of material and commentary written about it across books, news articles and websites. Some of the people responsible for these sources act as Operation Julie historians, albeit in an unofficial capacity.

I have detected in recent times a tendency to belittle or snipe away at the great success of this unique British police operation. You may feel it's natural given those circumstances, that I feel compelled to comment.

Much of this revisionism comes from sources that do not surprise me and they are almost all British. Mockery is one of many typical traits of the modern British psyche. What does surprise me are some derogatory comments seemingly originating from a handful of former detectives who enjoy picking and sniping.

I find it all a bit strange why this happens. None of these detractors, former cops or otherwise, were there. Many weren't even born in 1976. All this mockery and sniping from all sources is based on false information including false media reporting, rumours, innuendoes and downright conspiracy theories. Needless to say (I hope), I do not refer to the 'hunted' – those arrested because of the operation.

I remind you of what I wrote in the first chapter: I do not believe any kind of war existed back then. That became obvious to any onlooker at the time who could see the bond that developed between many of the drugs gang members and the detectives involved in Operation Julie – in many cases forged out of a mutual respect.

# ABOUT THE AUTHOR

Stephen Bentley is an award-winning author. Like some other authors, his life experience is broad and unconventional. He spent 30 years in the legal system, first as a detective for 15 years then as barrister plying his trade as 'a wig for hire' in London and the English provinces. He was a pioneering undercover cop on Operation Julie and as a barrister defended in trials involving murder, rape, drug importation, other serious crimes and defended soldiers at courts-martial.

He has now written over 20 books. Two of them have been optioned and are currently in development; one as a TV drama series, and one as a drama documentary.

His wife is a better person than him in all regards and is a source of support in his goal of entertaining readers. She has also made him a better person.

You can find Stephen and his book catalogue at stephenbentley.info

# BIBLIOGRAPHY

Black, David (2020) *Psychedelic Tricksters: A True Secret History of LSD* Independently Published

Black, David, *Psychedelic Tricksters: A True Secret History of LSD* (independently published, 2020)

Castaneda, Carlos, *The Teachings of Don Juan: A Yaqui Way of Knowledge*. The (University of California Press, 1968)

Ebenezer, Lyn, *Operation Julie: The World's Greatest LSD Bust* (Y Lolfa, 2015)

Fielding, Leaf, *To Live Outside the Law: Caught by Operation Julie* (Serpent's Tail, 2012)

Laxton, C. and Pritchard, M. *Busted! The Sensational Life-Story of an Undercover Hippie Cop* (Mirror Books Ltd., 1978)

Lee, D. and Pratt, C. *Operation Julie: How the Undercover Police Team Smashed the World's Greatest Drugs Ring* (W. H. Allen/Virgin Books, 1978)

Lewis, P. and Evans, R. *Undercover – The True Story of Britain's Secret Police* (Faber & Faber, 2016)

Tendler, S. and May, D. (1984). *Brotherhood of Eternal Love* (Panther Books, 1984)

# NOTES

1. BBC News, 'Operation Julie: How an LSD raid began the war on drugs' (12 Jul. 2011), https://bbc.in/300cZoA, accessed 16 Jul. 2017
2. Dick Fosbury was a 1968 Olympics Gold Medal high jump winner who perfected a new style of jumping.
3. BBC News, 'Operation Julie: Forty years since mid-Wales LSD bust' (10 Apr. 2016), http://www.bbc.com/news/uk-wales-35963741, accessed 16 Jul. 2017
4. Tendler, S. and May, D. (1984). *Brotherhood of Eternal Love* (Panther Books, 1984)
5. Five Bad Acid Trip Stories First Hand Experiences of LSD http://bit.ly/2ZYWPfb [can't find this one!]
6. Scouse is the name of the Liverpool dialect. A Scouser is a native of that city. Scouse is also a type of lamb or beef stew. The word comes from lobscouse, a stew commonly eaten by sailors throughout Northern Europe, which became popular in seaports such as Liverpool.
7. The Mau Mau Uprising, also known as the Mau Mau Rebellion, Mau Mau Revolt, or Kenya Emergency, was a military conflict that took place in British Kenya between 1952 and 1960.
8. *The Wire*, HBO (2002–08)
9. Castaneda, Carlos, *The Teachings of Don Juan: A Yaqui Way of Knowledge*. The (University of California Press, 1968)
10. There were only three undercover detectives at this stage. Andy Beaumont had returned to his home force a few months earlier.
11. Lee, D. and Pratt, C. *Operation Julie: How the Undercover Police Team Smashed the World's Greatest Drugs Ring* (W. H. Allen/Virgin Books, 1978)

12 'Old Cases' (Season 1, Episode 4), *The Wire*, HBO (2002–08), first broadcast 23 Jun. 2002.
13 I have since learned it was more likely to be a condition known as Dissociative Identity Disorder, which was unknown in the 1970s.
14 Tendler, S. and May, D. (1984) [Ibid at 4 above at page 160.
15 Ibid at 4 above at page 198.
16 Undercover Policing Inquiry (UCPI) https://www.ucpi.org.uk
17 BBC News, 'Undercover 'rulebook' published for the first time' (29 Jun. 2016), http://www.bbc.com/news/uk-36655666, accessed 16 Jul. 2017
18 European Union legislation governing working hours including those of goods vehicles' drivers
19 Ibid at 3 at page 3.